Benedikt Lorse

Warm-ups before singing
- The Handbook -
150 warm-ups for choirs and soloists

Bibliographic information by the German National Library: The German National Library lists this publication in the German National Bibliography; detailed bibliographic information can be found on the Internet on www.dnb.de.

Catalogue number: 2016001
ISBN 978-3-9817969-0-2

Translation from German into English: Anna Bonelli

© 2016 Fidelio –Verlag, Gerolstein

www.fidelio-verlag.de

The present work, including all of its parts, is protected by copyright. Any use beyond the boundaries of copyright law is inadmissible and punishable if without the consent of the publisher. This applies in particular to duplications, microfilming and processing in electronic systems.

Copyright notice:
Graphics for the individual exercises: © Ramona Kaulitzki - Fotolia.com

Index

Introduction		5
Why you should warm-up		7
I.	**Warm-ups for the body and rhythm**	10
	Exercises	10
	Practical advice: Rhythmic problems	18
II.	**Breathing**	19
	Short breathing theory	21
	Exercises	22
III.	**Humming**	27
	Exercises	28
	Practical advice:	
	What does it mean to slide up to a note?	32
IV.	**Ascending warm-up**	33
	Exercises	33
	Practical advice:	
	How can images influence our singing?	41
	Practical advice: Scat singing	47
	Practical advice: Commercial jingles	50
V.	**Descending warm-up**	52
	Exercises	52
	Piano or no piano? A question of tuning	56
VI.	**Diaphragmatic activation**	58
	Exercises	58
	Practical advice: Diaphragmatic activation	59

VII.	**Sound and vocal exercises**	**64**
	Exercises	64
	Changing tones chromatically – a simple exercise	69
VIII.	**Polyphonic sound exercises**	**71**
	Exercises	71
	All about your standing	79
IX.	**Rounds**	**83**
	Exercises	83
	Pronunciation makes the difference	86
	Call and Response, printed notes or Multimedia?	88
X.	**Simple popular folk songs**	**93**
	Practical advice:	
	How to give folk songs a modern twist	93
	Exercises	93
XI.	**Generic warm-up sequences**	**98**
	Possible warm-up: sequence 1	98
	Possible warm-up: sequence 2	104
	Possible warm-up: sequence 3	108

Warm-up before a performance	113
Protect your voice	114
What do professionals think of warming up?	115

Introduction:

*Warming up must be fun and motivational for
the next choir rehearsal.*

We all know it, we all do it, but for most of us, it's just an annoying matter of duty of each weekly choir rehearsal: having to warm-up before the actual start of the choir rehearsal. Apropos, it's the same for singers and choir director.

This does not mean that annoying obligations can't be fun. Actually, there are countless variations and funny little songs that are easy to enjoy and can even increase motivation.

Anyhow, warming up can only be fun and enjoyable if we know why or how we have to do it and if we dispose sufficient exercises and variations, which can render the start of the rehearsal diversified.

In current literature, it's quite common to read that one can tell a good choir and a good choirmaster from the warm-up. Warm-ups should work towards the rehearsal, take pressure from certain passages, and match later parts. For professional choirs, that may be true, but for the many thousands of recreational and amateur choirs that characterize the majority of the choir scene, however, this is completely unrealistic. First of all, most choir directors work part-time, have another job, or do not have enough time to meticulously prepare each rehearsal, and second, warming up would actually become an annoying and boring duty.

This is where this book starts. The book is compiled from practice for practice and, particularly, intended for recreational choirs. It's not about conveying deep voice training. It should, rather, show different ways of organizing warm-ups. Technical terms are, therefore, largely unnecessary. Warming up should be fun. That's why many fun and intense exercises are added to the work. Of course, classic exercises shouldn't be missed, but they should and must be agreeable to the choir and the choirmaster. Consider this book as support and inspiration, not as a mere manual. Change all exercises, so they can fit your choir. Diversify, try to have courage to implement your own ideas.

Last but not least, a small note: For the sake of legibility and clarity, only the masculine form is used in this book. So if choral conductors or singers are mentioned, as a matter of course, all women are included.

Benedikt Lorse   Gerolstein, May 2015

> **Consideration:** All composite chord symbols in this book correspond to the international system (American model), which means that the German H is noted as B, and the B as Bb.

Why you should warm-up

Warming up before the beginning of a rehearsal has various goals; three of which should be discussed in detail. However, the meaning and the importance of the various goals vary from choir to choir and can't be described as standard.

a) **Warming up as a starting ritual**
Very important points in any group dynamic are rituals and routine. Especially in a choir, which often stands in a big contrast to daily routine, it is absolutely necessary to create a certain attunement. Choir rehearsals often take place in the evenings on workdays because of practical reasons. Therefore, they are usually preceded by a stressful day of work or other duties of everyday life. As an example, we could take a family man, who left home in the morning to get to his job in the company he works for, who spent the day in meetings or talking to clients, picked up his children after work, shortly discussed the holiday arrangements with his wife, and then rushed to the choir rehearsal. It is understandable that this man might need a smooth transition before having to focus for two hours straight on a possibly complicated choir performance. This often happens to many singers. Warming up covers this transition. It's all about creating that certain ambiance that helps choir members to focus on their task. Following these reflections, an effective warm-up should be organized. Start with something very calm and quiet, i.e. with breathing exercises.

Hum for a little bit and slowly increase the intensity. When the singers have reached a calm state of mind and are ready to focus on the following tasks, you can start with the actual rehearsal.

b) Warm-up to prepare

Far more often, warming up is understood as simple preparation. The voice, the vocal cords, and the entire vocal tract can be seen as a large muscle that needs to be activated slowly and gently before having to work hard. Any athlete knows, before the actual training, warming up is necessary in order to prepare the muscles, prevent injury, and get ready for the coming burden. No one would do a 100 m sprint or similar exercises without previous preparation. The same can be applied to the voice. Light, simple exercises, therefore, are well-suited to prepare the voice for the coming tasks.

c) Warming up as voice training

In literature, the voice formation function of warming up is the most described. Accordingly, in the first phase, phonation is mainly operated. Voice training means teaching vocal techniques, facts about the vocal tract, and forms of an individual choir sound. Since most people have their own intrinsic concept of voice and singing, which has crystallized over many years in everyday life, it is very costly and time-consuming to change these ideas and to shape the voice. Therefore, a lot of time is needed to produce a noticeable change in sound by voice training. Therefore, it is necessary to regularly complete units on this aspect, at best, at every rehearsal. The phonation aspect can only be transferred with difficulty to all choirs, because basic requirements are needed and not every choir can meet them. The choirmaster has to have some experience in the field if he wants to carry out these units, and he should have great knowledge on vocal techniques and the appropriate didactics. Very few choirs can afford a private vocal coach or singing teacher.

Anyhow, phonation isn't only necessary to overcome every day concepts of voice and singing, but also to create a unified choral sound. A common question is whether choir and solo singers differ. Many vocal coaches negate this, and technically, they are right. The vocal techniques are the same, in a choir or as a soloist. There are many techniques and tricks you can learn in order to achieve a firm, clear voice with a large scale. This doesn't depend on the form of singing. However, choral singing goes one step further. A choir should be mostly perceived as an overall sound, where individual voices blend. However, this can only be achieved if all singers can rely on the same concepts and attitudes. That's why choral vocal training is necessary, since it fulfils this objective. A good example is different vocal colours. Each vowel can resound open or closed, light or dark. Different vowel colours can directly cause intonation problems and other kinds of interference. Therefore, it is very important to find a common attitude in any kind of choral vocal training; vocal and sound exercises are ideal for this purpose.

As mentioned at the beginning, the focalization on the aforementioned points differs from choir to choir. The voice formation aspect is, perhaps, more likely to apply to professional choirs and ambitious amateur choirs, while getting ready and into the mood applies to the majority of recreational choirs. Of course, both aspects are always ideal goals. A stressed choir member will be able to participate at a rehearsal, even without warming up. It is no obligation, but it helps immensely.

How long should a good warm-up last?
The question of how long a decent warm-up should last causes a lot of discussion, and you will hear countless different opinions. There are choirmasters who are ok with five minutes, and there are choirmasters who extend the initial session to up to 30 minutes. It always depends on the individual choir, the intention of the choirmaster, and on the goals, in particular. Of course, a choir that has warmed up for a long time will be better prepared and, perhaps, will sing better and more purely than a choir who has warmed up for five minutes only. But the latter will have an extra 25 minutes to practice on the pieces. Therefore, it's always a cost-benefit calculation. Long warm-ups take up a lot of rehearsal time, which might miss at the end.
In addition, it certainly always depends on what phase is being practiced.
If a concert is coming up soon, a long warm-up can make perfect sense to optimally prepare intonation, timbre, and volume in order to achieve an optimum chorus sound. If a rehearsal is used to develop a new piece, it is probably of secondary importance to warm-up perfectly, as long as it comes to the pure study of the notes, and the singers are trying to pronounce a Swedish text for the first time. In such a case, even the longest warm-up would not help.

I. Warm-ups for the body and rhythm

Body warm-ups, generally, fulfil two main functions: They raise awareness and sensitivity for one's own body, which is an important factor when singing, and they help the "arrival" at the beginning of a rehearsal. Many choir rehearsals in the leisure and amateur area are held in the evening during the week. The singers probably had a stressful day and other challenges behind them. Therefore, it is often difficult to start without a smooth transition towards an intense and difficult choir rehearsal. Moreover, simple body warm-ups can also stretch and loosen the muscles that are involved in singing. It is certainly possible to discuss vocal benefits and costs-use statements, but as an initial ritual and physical match, they have proven their worth.

Body warm-ups

Exercise 1: Describe circles with shoulders

Make circles with your shoulders, forward and backwards. Start with the right shoulder first, forward and then backward. Repeat the same exercise with the left shoulder. Then let both shoulders circle together, first forward, then backward. It's quite difficult to circle forward with one shoulder and backwards with the other one.

Exercise 2: Walk on the spot

Start to slowly walk on the spot and become faster and faster, until you're actually running. Get slower and repeat the exercise once more.

Exercise 3: The pendulum

Oscillate forwards and backwards with your body, as well as to the left and to the right, while standing firmly on the floor.

Exercise 4: Chew and yawn

Perform comfortable chewing movements. Yawn extensively. Then caress your cheeks and massage your jaw muscles.

Exercise 5: Grasp the sky

Raise your arms above your head and stretch them out as far as possible. Then gently bend forward to the right and then to the left side until you feel a slight sense of expansion in your side.

Exercise 6: Flutter your lips

Let your lips flutter while you completely relax and exhale. Depending on the size of the room and the space between the individual singers, it may be a good idea to keep a hand over the mouth during this exercise.

Exercise 7: Circle your feet

It is not that easy to stand on one leg for a long time. It's even more difficult when you stand on one leg and let the other foot circle around its hinge. Tip: Focus on the little toe of the foot. It helps to maintain the balance.

Exercise 8: Shake off routine

Shake arms and legs. Proceed slowly and decrease the body portion that is to be shaken. For example, first shake the whole arm, then only the hand, and then each single finger. The same can also be done with legs and feet.

Exercise 9: Forget everyday life

Forget the worries of your everyday life. Caress, tap on your body, and massage it from head to feet while you get rid of your problems.

Exercise 10: The compass

Stretch out your arms on either side of the body and turn them left and right alternately. Important: The feet remain anchored to the floor all the time.

Exercise 11: Hang your head

Bend forward and let your head, arms, and torso relax in a hanging position. Please slowly straighten up along your spine. At last, also straighten your head.

Exercise 12: Nosepainting

Write words in the air, using your nose. This exercise helps perceive your body with more sensibility.

Exercise 13: Rising sun

Inhale and rise your arms above your head. Stretch and let your arms represent a ball (sun) on the outside.

Exercise 14: Circle your head

Perform circular movements with your head, once in one direction, the next time in the opposite one. Be careful and perform this exercise with caution, to prevent injuries.

Rhythm exercises

Rhythm exercises are not only exciting warm-ups, which bind the singers at the beginning of a rehearsal, they also fulfil other purposes. On one hand, rhythms are trained; of course, on the other hand, they also serve as a conscious focus on the choirmaster, since they are mostly conducted by call-and-response. The simplest form is where the choirmaster claps a rhythm, and the choir has to repeat it. It is recommended to comply with the meter when changing between choir and choral conductor, i.e. the two groups should clap in time. It might be a good idea to let a metronome run during the whole exercise. Clapping in a group can cause big speed deviations. Some rhythms are shown in the following part; they can be used in this order. Of course, there are countless other rhythms, beats, and time signatures that you can try. Therefore, the following information is only one idea, and it should encourage you to implement your own ideas.

Exercise 1: One beat rhythm

Warm-ups for the body and rhythm 15

Exercise 2: Two beat rhythm

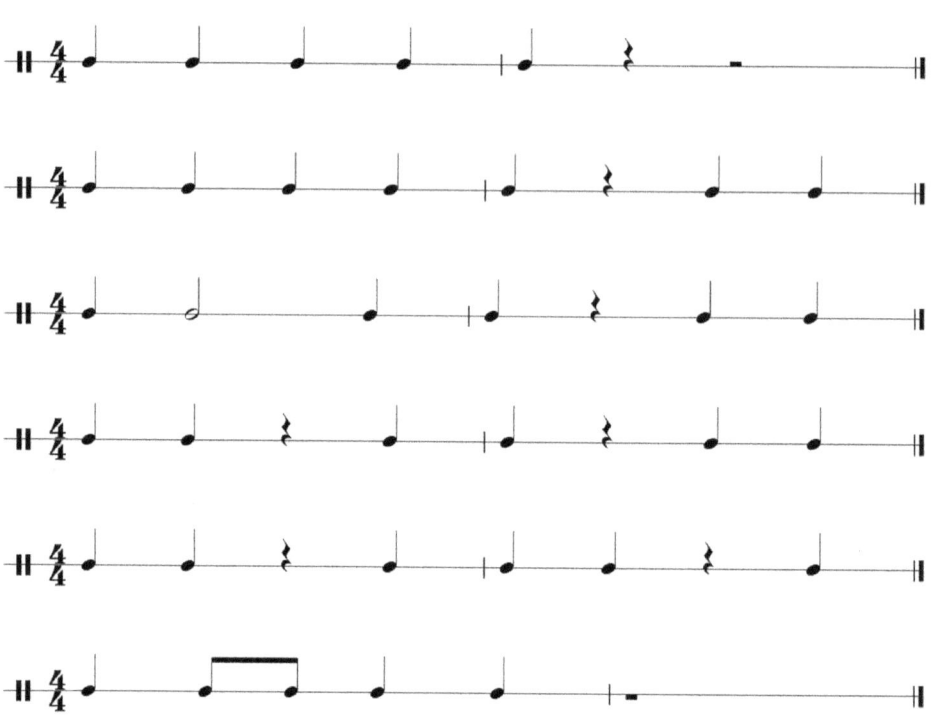

16   Warm-ups for the body and rhythm

Practical advice: Rhythmic problems

Nothing causes as many rhythmical problems as trying to clap in unison. Choirs usually get faster and faster, which might also happen when doing the aforementioned exercises. With fast rhythms in particular choirs may also happen to clap too slowly. This often happens because the clapping is done ineffectively. Only a small gesture is actually needed to clap - the hands do not have to move far apart. But many singers prefer rather large, decaying arm movements. This means that the hands won't be able to join each other again. Large, expansive movements are often a major reason for imprecise clapping.

And what if the choir gets faster? Take a slow 4/4-beat exercise and set a metronome. Always clap on beat 1 of the metronome. Halve the speed of the metronome and keep counting, you'll hear the sound of the metronome only every second beat. You can now continue with this arbitrarily. The pilot tone of the metronome will be heard less and less. However, you must continue to count in time. This is how a consistent pace can be rehearsed. Since smartphones are widely used nowadays, singers could think of downloading a metronome app and performing the exercises alone: on the bus, on the train or anywhere else. Clapping is not even necessary to do this. A tap on one leg or even the pure mental follow-up is sufficient.

More effective rhythm exercises can be found under the heading "body percussion". When using body percussions, the body is used as percussion set to produce different sounds. Clapping, tapping on the chest or on other parts of the body can produce some very complex rhythms, especially in groups.

II. Breathing

Breathing is considered an important pillar in singing. It is more difficult, however, to explain this to a choir, so that it doesn't only understand it, but also puts it into practice. Probably, there is no general concept to teach the choir how to breath efficiently. But there are exercises and methods that help establish breathing as an important part of singing.

Main problem

The main problem in the teaching of breathing techniques lies in the fact that breathing while singing differs quite a lot from normal, everyday breathing. During the day, the duration of inhalations and exhalations is mostly the same, even if, on some occasions, inhalations are longer. When singing, it works exactly the other way around. A lot of air has to be inhaled in a short period of time, but then, it gets out slowly over a long period of time (while singing). Since the time people spend singing is relatively low for most people, our everyday concept of breathing outweighs the other, even if one knows the difference in theory.

Possible solutions

Therefore, it is important to clarify the difference between every day breathing and breathing while singing. Generally, there are two proven concepts to convey such techniques:

a) Continuous repetitions

The importance of breathing should be constantly emphasized and practiced. Only when breathing exercises are performed regularly during warm-ups, the choir will be able to internalize these concepts and use them. Single priority hours or workshops are certainly helpful to intensely treat the matter, but it is questionable how long the learned techniques will last. Continuous exercises are usually required for a lasting effect.

b) The practical experience of differences

Practical experience is better than any theory. Let your choir hear and feel how different breathing techniques can cause differences in the sound. It works especially well with very harmonious, wide, and evocative sequences. Let the choir first sing without any particular instruction. Then, ask it to breathe consciously. The essence of conscious breathing is to be explained in detail on the next page. You are guaranteed to generate a huge sonic difference. It is secondary and hard to tell if this, ultimately, is due to a change in breathing, or rather, to the higher concentration produced. Conscious breathing always produces a purer and fuller sound.

Short breathing theory

More complex processes are involved in breathing: the lungs, the trachea with the larynx as a conclusion, the diaphragm, the intercostals muscles, and the abdominal and back muscles. The diaphragm plays a special role. The diaphragm muscle is a band, which lies horizontally in the body and separates the abdomen from the chest cavity. Attached to the diaphragm, there are the lungs. The lung, itself, is not a muscle and can't expand and contract itself. This task is performed by the diaphragm. When it descends, the chest cavity expands so that air can get in. The activity of the diaphragm can be seen on the abdominal wall. When the stomach bulges outward, this is a visible sign of the lowering of the diaphragm, which presses the organs slightly outwards. This way of breathing is called **diaphragmatic respiration**. However, the chest cavity can also be expanded with the help of the intercostals muscles. For this purpose, the lower ribcage (the lower ribs) expand outwards, thus creating a widening. This way of breathing is called **thoracic respiration.**

When singing, people usually use a mixture of the two breathing exercises in order to breathe in as much air as possible, and at the same time, allow a constant air outlet (strut). For respiration in a choir, the following instructions can be given on breathing: The air should flow in easily, not be sucked in a cramped way. Figuratively speaking, the body should fill with air from the bottom. First, the air flows deeply into the abdomen, then laterally into the ribs, and then it causes an erection in the front part of the chest. Make sure not to breathe in too much, as to lift the shoulders convulsively. This only leads to a debilitating airway closure. To use another image, if the air gets just below the shoulder, it is sufficient.

Exercises

There are countless different breathing techniques and exercises to rehearse this. Here, we describe just a few basic exercises that are suitable for everyday rehearsals.

Exercise 1: Cherry pie with cream

Close your eyes and imagine the delicious smell of a cherry pie with cream. Alternatively, of course, you can think of any other dish that makes your mouth water.
Now, breathe in this soothing smell, deeply through your nose. Change your focus gradually. After you have absorbed the smell twice without instructions, be careful and lead the smell to the abdomen, gradually filling the space of the rib cage, the abdomen and your chest with the smell. All this should happen with the calmness with which you suck in the smell of cherry pie and cream on a quiet Sunday afternoon.

Exercise 2: Hard times

Breathe in deeply through your mouth and let the air out with a big, huge sigh. Let your body follow this action by slightly crumpling. Repeat this exercise several times.

Exercise 3: Nothing but hot soup

Cool an imaginary spoon of soup by repeatedly blowing on it. Perform this action as you would every day. Inhale without thinking about it, blow, inhale once again, and blow one more time.

Exercise 4: Balloon

Breathe in deeply, following the above-described pattern, and let the air escape slowly and constantly. The aim is to achieve the longest possible and constant airflow. Measure the time and compare the records to see if there has been an improvement between rehearsals.

The exercise can be performed in different versions on different sounds. Each consonant, thereby, has a different mouth opening and different difficulty.

This exercise seems to work even better when it is performed while lying down. Whoever puts his hand on the abdomen just below the ribs may consciously feel the inhalation.

Variant a)

Variant b)

Variant c)

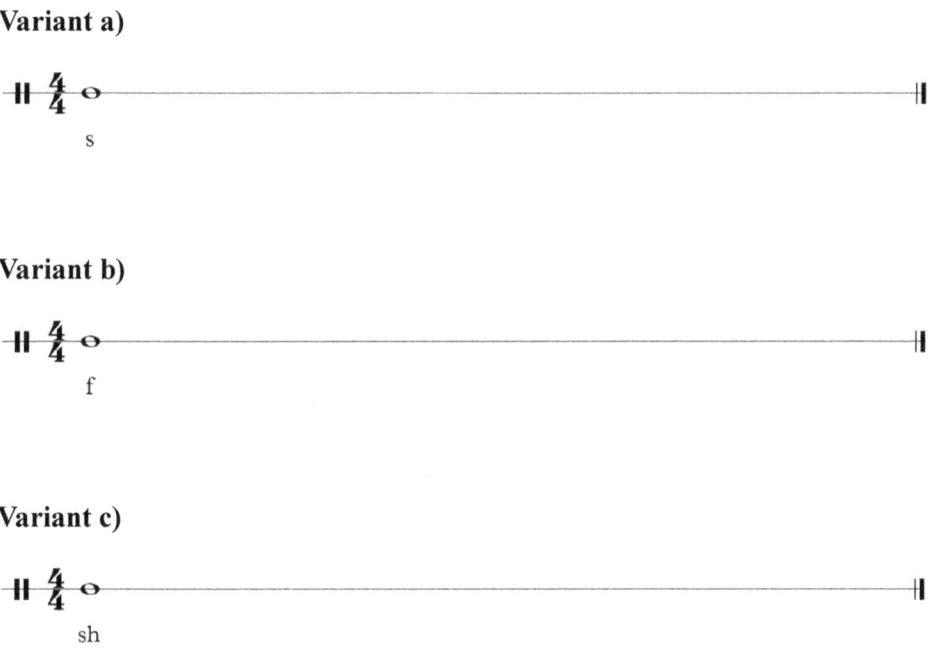

Exercise 5: Locomotive

The diaphragm isn't only important during inspiration, but also in exhalation. Especially when singing, the support given by the diaphragm muscle is of great importance.

This can be practiced with short, powerful sounds with a conscious use of the diaphragm. Initially, the variant is "f-s-sh", as it allows a soft start. However, also "p-t-k" is suitable for this exercise.

Variant a)
Slow start with softer f, s, and sh

Variant b)
Harder consonants p, t and k

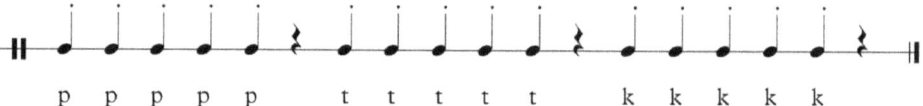

Exercise 6

In order to increase the speed and train the ability in articulating, you can try the following exercise. Start slowly and get faster and faster.

Variant a)
This time, the sounds "p", "t" and "k" are softer, since less air has to be used for them, and one has to concentrate less on breathing, as a consequence.

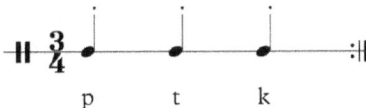

p   t   k

Variant b)
More difficult variant with "f", "s" and "sh"

f   s   sh

Variation:

Instead of performing f-s-sh or p-t-k in a specified order, this can also be done when recognising a given sign. Establish a sign or a gesture for each single sound, for example, a flat hand that perpendicularly intersects the air for s, a horizontal movement for sh, and a fist that moves forward for sch. As the choirmaster, you will decide how often a sound has to be performed. Your choir is forced to attentive watching.

Breathing

Exercise 7

Please be careful to perform the following exercise evenly, both in pace and dynamic.

Variant a)

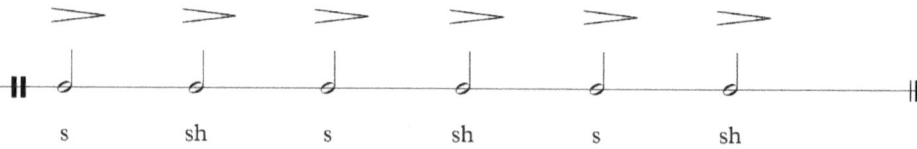

Variant b)

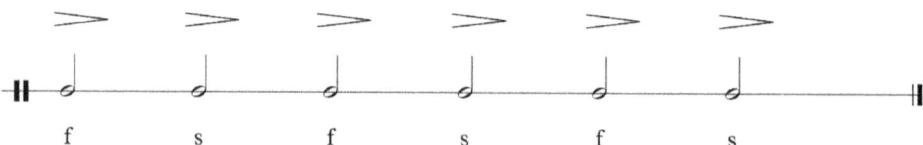

Variant c)

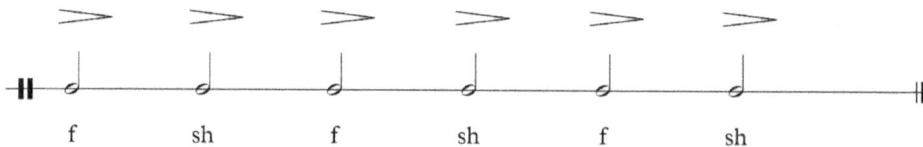

III. Humming

To hum at the beginning of each rehearsal before singing with vowels, syllables, or entire texts has a number of advantages that are not only of voice-physiological nature.

Humming is quiet
As humming is a quiet procedure, it helps improve concentration. The effects are similar to meditation. Thus, it forms a counterpoint to the often noisy and hectic everyday life. Just like body percussions or body warm-ups, it is useful in the ritual of focussing and gaining concentration.

Humming is easy
For most people, it is difficult to focus on different aspects simultaneously. Singing is unlikely complex in its diversity. Breathing, vowel formation, texts, pitch, volume, posture, and even more elements must be considered simultaneously. Humming eliminates a few things straightaway, so it becomes easier to focus on single points. For example, prior to starting to hum, the choir could be instructed to focus on breathing.

Humming makes the body swing
Humming brings the body to vibrate internally more than any other type of tone generation. Thus, the perception of the body is strengthened.

Humming frees

Nothing frees vocal cords better than humming. The uniform vibration that is caused by humming gently and sustainably removes any kind of issue. Clearing your voice, as usual, when it is husky, however, has exactly the opposite effect. The vocal cords bash against each other. The following irritation causes a rapid formation of more problems.

Humming as self-assessment

Humming is an important indicator of vocal problems. If the voice is healthy, humming is a very pleasant activity, where vocal cords can vibrate easily and without obstacles. If you notice any kind of problem while humming (low ambit, high fatigue, not so clear tone), it could be a sign of wrong posture or wrong respiration. A vocal instructor will be able to help you in this case.

Exercises

Always start your humming exercises very slowly. In the end, it is all about singing together for the first time during the rehearsal. For this reason, even very easy pauses are enough at the beginning. Be careful to hum in a relaxed way. Humming should always be performed with a certain calm and tranquillity.

Exercise 1

Variant a)

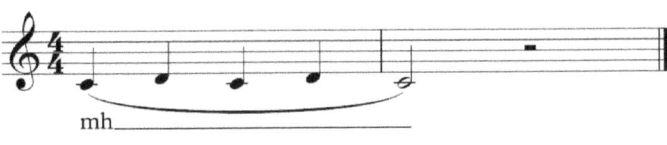

↗ Chromatically upwards

Variant b)
Alternatively, you can even add a fifth at the end.

↗ Chromatically upwards

Exercise 2

Generally, fifths are much harder to sing than what one would actually think. Singing with a particularly good intonation to get to a very clean interval is not that easy. For this reason, it might be good to sing a few fifths as a start.

↗ Chromatically upwards

Humming

Exercise 3

Be careful to actually sing Legato during this tone sequence. The single tones shouldn't be hit singularly.

Variant a)

mh_____

↗ Chromatically upwards

Variant b)

Alternatively, you can add a fifth at the end once more.

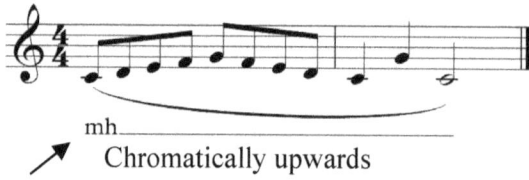

mh_____

↗ Chromatically upwards

Variant c)

mh_____

↗ Chromatically upwards

Exercise 4

Also, this exercise should be sung Legato, without hitting each single tone once again.

Variant a)

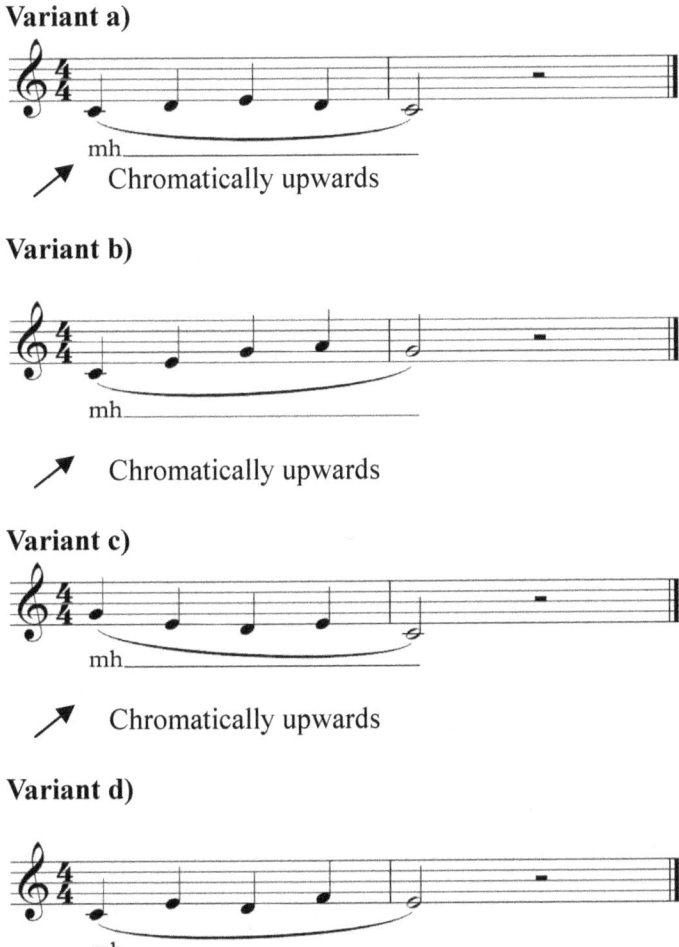

Chromatically upwards

Variant b)

Chromatically upwards

Variant c)

Chromatically upwards

Variant d)

Chromatically upwards

Exercise 5

In this exercise, the tone scale is sung by going back to the basic tone all the time. Whet the tones consciously; don't move directly to the tone you are trying to reach.

Practical advice: What does it mean to *slide up to a note?*

In musical theory sliding up to a note means beginning a tone with the help of other tones. Most sounds are slid up to from below. The sound isn't hit directly, since the lower tones are sung one after the other until the target sound has been reached. The whole thing happens very quickly, but is still audible and may even cause the sound of the choir to be negative.

Nevertheless, it might even be useful when warming up, since all tones are covered and a uniform vibration of the voice may be maintained more easily. However, these techniques should be used consciously and not be transferred to the rest of the rehearsal.

IV. Ascending warm-up

It corresponds to a general logic that warm-up exercises should always be started in a vocal range that can be managed without effort. Gradually, you can then advance to the outlying area and stress and strengthen them with continuous exercise. For close set warm-up exercises, therefore, a start in C-Major is usually the best option, for multi-tone exercises, it would be A-Major. Of course, this can vary from choir to choir.

Another option is to split the voices and make an internal differentiation. This way, you can start with the warm-up exercises that begin in A major, initially, only with bass. From C major, you can then add the tenor and the soprano. The same would apply for the high notes. Beyond a certain limit, only the tenor and the soprano would then sing.

This form makes warm-ups complicated, requires a higher concentration and, therefore, can represent a demanding improvement.

Easy exercises in close position

Exercise 1

a) na na na   ...
b) la la la   ...
c) ma ma ma ...

➚ Chromatically upwards

Exercise 2: Morning feeling

a) na na na ...
b) la la la ...
c) ma ma ma ...

↗ Chromatically upwards

Exercise 3: Football stadium

The following exercise is a great way to show your choir which volume it can achieve. It is perfectly normal if you can't control very loud sounds and quiet sounds, which are particularly severe in their intonation, compared to the average volume levels. Therefore, some choirs and choir masters tend to not entirely exploit their vocal potential. Nevertheless, sometimes, it is necessary to achieve a high volume in the choir. To gain a sense of what is possible, fan chants from the football area are a proven means. What is it about in the stadium, if not to drown rival fans with the high volume of our songs?

o - lé,   o - lé - o - lé - o - é

↗ Chromatically upwards

Exercise 4

The following exercise is a simple relaxation exercise for lips and voices. Try to complete this exercise without tension and stiffness.

a) mi - ni - mi - ni ...
b) nu - mu - nu - mu ...
c) me - ne - me - ne ...
d) mo - mo - mo - mo ...
e) lo - lo - lo - lo ...

↗ Chromatically upwards

Exercise 5

The exercise should be carried out in quite a fast pace then become successively faster. The pace is correct if the syllables are still articulated clearly and cleanly.

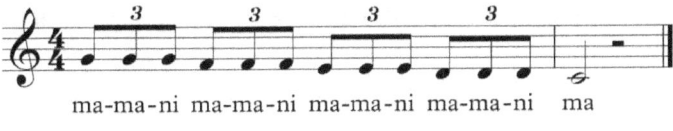

ma-ma-ni ma-ma-ni ma-ma-ni ma-ma-ni ma

↗ Chromatically upwards

Ascending warm-up

Exercise 6

This exercise doesn't only loosen lips and voices, but it also trains the breath and a regular air flow.

Variant a)
Repeat the exercise three times without breathing in the meantime.

a) mo mo mo ...
b) ma ma ma ...

↗ Chromatically upwards

Variant b)

a) mo mo mo ...
b) ma ma ma ...

↗ Chromatically upwards

Exercise 7

La - bel - lo, La - bel - lo. La - bel - lo, La - bel - lo, La - bel - lo, La - bel - lo, La - bel - lo

↗ Chromatically upwards

Exercise 8

Electricity and *electricity station* are two words where a lot of "C" and "T" are repeated in a short time. Thus, they are suitable to illustrate the interplay of consonants and vowels. It is possible to sing tunefully only on vowels. This is the ideal of classical singing. However, in pop and jazz singing, one often wants the opposite. But it is impossible to sing on sounds like "K" and "T". Therefore, the following exercise is about completing the vowels and using the consonants only to form words.

Variant a)

➚ Chromatically upwards

Variant b)

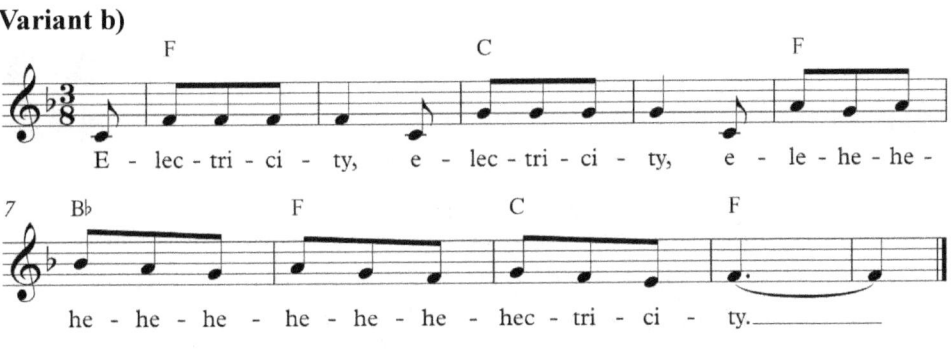

➚ Chromatically upwards

Ascending warm-up

Tetrads and other exercises above an octave

The German word, *Sonne (engl. sun)*, probably is the most famous word in warm-up exercises in German singing theory. This because of the open "O" [ɔ:] that the word *Sonne* contains and the final soft "N". It can also be very easy to vary, which can be a great advantage. With an "A" [a:], we immediately obtain the word *Sahne (engl. cream)*, which is easier to sing at higher pitches.

Exercise 9

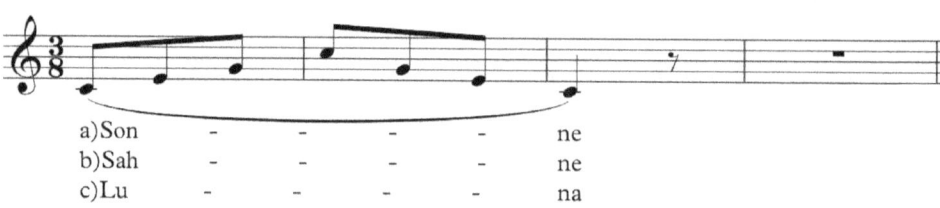

a) Son - - - - ne
b) Sah - - - - ne
c) Lu - - - - na

 Chromatically upwards

Exercise 10

Perform the following exercise by using the diaphragm.

a) die So, die So, die Son - ne
b) die Sah, die Sah, die Sah - ne

 Chromatically upwards

Ascending warm-up

Exercise 11

The following exercises should be performed with a lot of sound. Be careful to sing legato on vowels, so they are sung as one, long continuous vowel. Otherwise, it is very easy to transform *Son-ne* or *Sah-ne* in So-ho-ho-honne or Sa-ha-ha-hahne.

Variant a)

↗ Chromatically upwards

Variant b)

↗ Chromatically upwards

Variant c)

↗ Chromatically upwards

Ascending warm-up

Variant d)

↗ Chromatically upwards

Variant e)

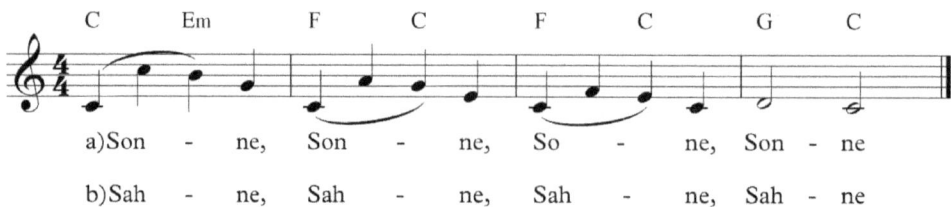

↗ Chromatically upwards

Variant f)

↗ Chromatically upwards

Variant g)

↗ Chromatically upwards

Variant h)

↗ Chromatically upwards

Variant i)

↗ Chromatically upwards

Practical advice: How can images influence our singing?

There are several ways to give a choir an idea of a sound. One can explain the theoretical mouth positions or show sample recordings. However, the simplest method is to use mental images. Try to convey a visual impression of a sound to the singers of your choir. *Think of raindrops* or *think of a rising sun* are very specific comparisons in this context. But even more extreme images can be used when warming up. Let the choir sing like an opera singer or quack like a duck. Have the singers breathe like the wind and roar like a lion. Only who knows the extreme positions will know how locate between them.

Exercise 12

Complete this exercise by using your diaphragm. To do this, put your fingers on your belly, just below the ribs. When you breathe in deeply, you will perceive a certain movement with your fingers. Alternatively, you can also try to "teeter" your fingers by using your diaphragm. Afterwards, you can perform the following exercise.

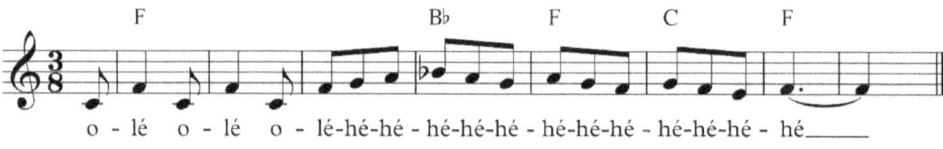

↗ Chromatically upwards

Exercise 13

Convey a very energetic and resolute image to fill the following exercise with life. Once again, try to use the diaphragm.

↗ Chromatically upwards

Exercise 14

The following exercise is beyond the scope of an octave and, therefore, should be performed only after several other warm-ups.

↗ Chromatically upwards

Exercise 15

↗ Chromatically upwards

Ascending warm-up

Exercise 16

Convey the image of a swarming, licentious Italian.

↗ Chromatically upwards

Exercise 17

Convey the opposite to Exercise 16. Curse as much as you can, like a clichéd Italian.

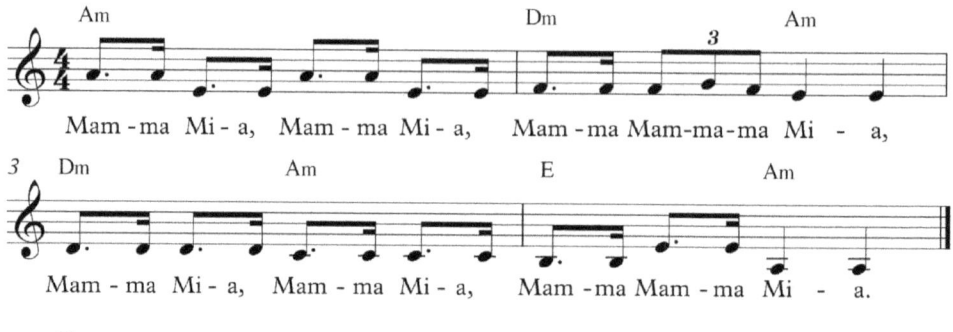

↗ Chromatically upwards

Exercise 18: Country canon

The following exercise, the *Country canon,* can be used as a canon, as well as a simple, melodic warm-up. Pay attention to the swing rhythm.

↗ Chromatically upwards

Exercise 19: Tomato salad

The following exercise is loosening and, usually, renders everybody enthusiastic right from the start. The word, tomato salad, is always stressed in a different way. In the usual pronunciation, the emphasis is on the second syllable: to<u>ma</u>to salad. In the following exercises, the emphasis keeps going one syllable backwards. It can make sense to speak out the exercise once before starting:
To<u>ma</u>to salad - toma<u>to</u> salad - tomato sa<u>lad</u> - tomato sa<u>lad</u> - to<u>ma</u>to salad - toma<u>to</u> salad - tomato <u>sa</u>lad - tomato sa<u>lad</u>.

Ascending warm-up

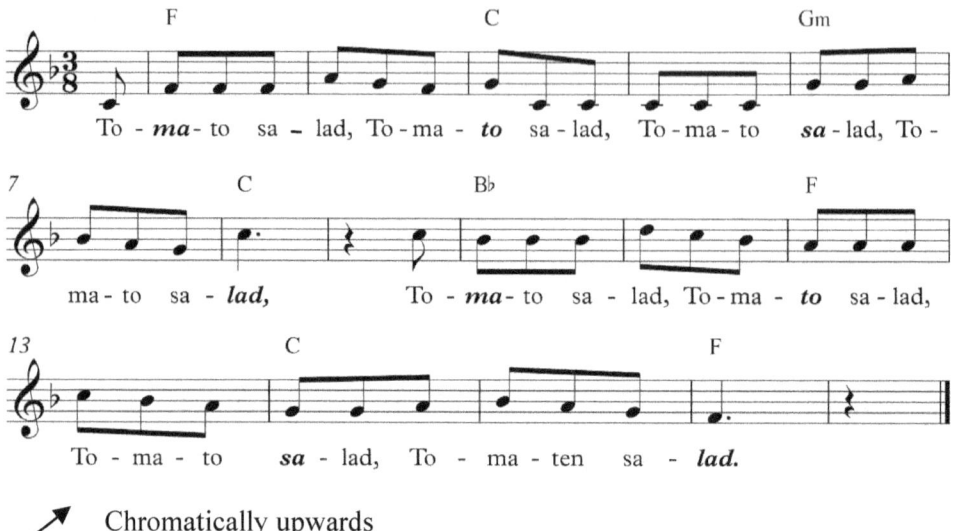

↗ Chromatically upwards

Exercise 20

↗ Chromatically upwards

Ascending warm-up

Practical advice: Scat singing

Scat referred to jazz and gospel singing is a special form of singing, where syllables or words with no discernible meaning are rhythmically and melodically put together. *Scat singing* originally served simple vocal improvisation. Meanwhile, however, scat syllables are often used in jazz and pop arrangements. Known syllables include, but are not limited to da, bob, dl, dn, dwee, dooh, bab and many others. The pronunciation and spelling usually vary from author to author. Usually, however, a double "e" (e.g. dwee) is pronounced [i:] and a double "o" (e.g. ooh) like [u:]. Of particular importance are final consonants. A "b" at the end of a syllable (e.g. bab) isn't generally spoken out, since it merely serves the clean finish of the vowel. Since it is very hard to find a precise conclusion on a vowel, the mouth closes on a "b", but without making a sound. Thus, precise endings are made possible even with a larger number of singers. One of the best-known living scat artists is Kirby Shaw.

The first use of scat singing is not really known. Louis Armstrong spread the story that he was the first who recorded scat singing in 1926, when the notes mistakenly fell to the ground during a recording. He had to improvise and make use of scat syllables. However, previous recordings of the use of scat syllables have already emerged, so the story of Louis Armstrong was unmasked as a legend.

Scat singing doesn't only serve simple improvisation. One may also deliberately try to imitate vocal instruments. That's how many jazz arrangements manage to convey a very good imitation of whole big band sounds through the skilful use of light and dark vowels (e.g. du-ba).

Exercise 21

The following exercise is a contrast exercise between staccato and legato passages. Ensure the staccato points are sung very quickly, and the Legato parts are actually linked and sung without re-starting. The difficulty lies in enduring this change over time.

↗ Chromatically upwards

Exercise 22

Exercise 22 is an exercise with simple scat syllables. You should also read the above practical tip "scat syllables".
The difficulty of the exercise lies in the rhythm. The eighth notes of the second row must be short, but still sung exactly in time. Many choirs tend to be too fast and to shorten the breaks in passages like this.

Ascending warm-up

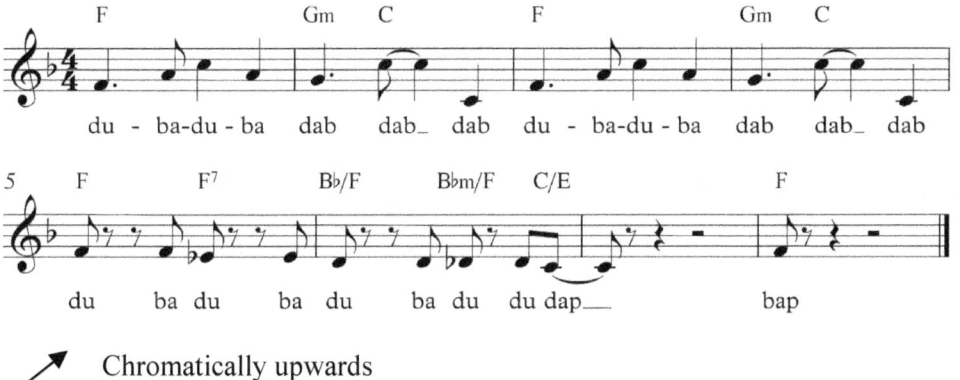

↗ Chromatically upwards

Exercise 23

You can easily use Scat-syllables in a playful way. Be careful to cleanly end the syllables and pay attention to the swing rhythm.

Variant a)

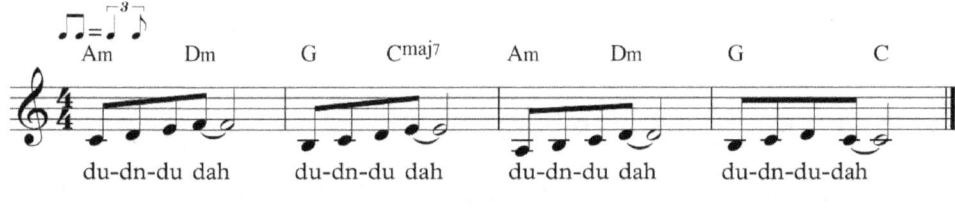

↗ Chromatically upwards

Variant b)

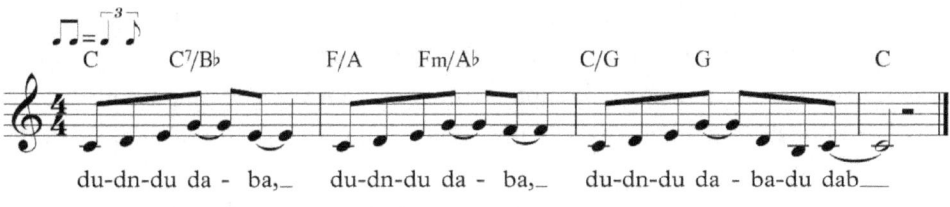

↗ Chromatically upwards

Ascending warm-up

Variant c)

↗ Chromatically upwards

Variant d)

↗ Chromatically upwards

Practical advice: Commercial jingles

Simple melodies and funny chords are often played during warm ups, since these little melodies are really catchy, simple and quite easy to reproduce.

Exactly the same also applies to commercial jingles and theme songs from TV shows, where a high recognition value and short, concise melodies are desired. The most brilliant advertising jingle in what regards memorability and brand recognition probably is the jingle of Telekom, which consists of exactly 5 tones and a single interval: a major third. So why not use commercial jingles when warming up? Everyone in your choir will know them and be able to sing them directly. In addition to that, they often act like a motivational miracle. That's why you should use the theme of Hornbach, The Simpsons, Danny cream, kid shows or similar jingles at the beginning of your rehearsal.

Due to copyright concerns the notes can't be printed in this book, for you however, this is no problem.

Exercise 24: Oh happy day

The exercise, *Oh happy day,* is a simple scale and interval exercise. However, it receives a certain gospel touch during its course. A similar tone sequence also appears in the Gospel, *Oh happy day,* from the movie, *Sister Act II*. The exercise is designed to be bipolar. Each part is repeated. It is advisable, therefore, to carry out the exercise call-and-response. However, this must not only consist of an interchange between the choral conductor and the choir. There are countless ways to organize such an antiphon. Possibilities include splitting the choir into two or more small groups to share, where either a fixed group has to start or the selection occurs on call. In a chorus where there is a good group feeling, it's also possible to select individuals who start singing

In the last cycle of the exercise, the specified chords represent an opportunity to make chromatic key changes.

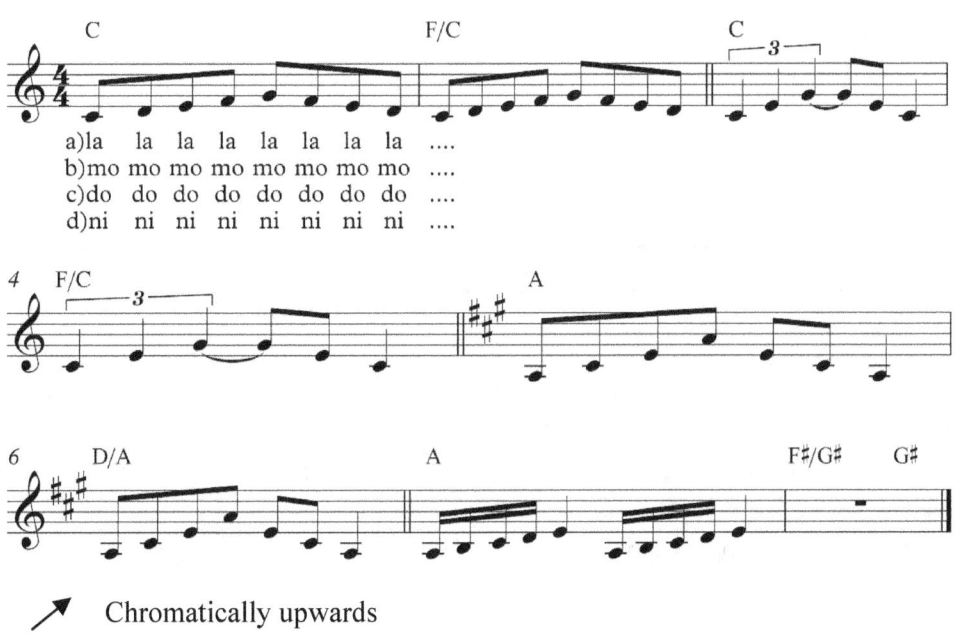

↗ Chromatically upwards

Ascending warm-up

V. Descending warm-up

Most people find it easier to sing low notes than high notes if they don't warm-up beforehand. In fact, high tones are more difficult. The explanation is that the vocal cords vibrate in a very relaxed way when they produce low tones. As in a deep guitar string, the voltage is low, and the frequency is very low; consequently, the sound is low. After prolonged singing, many people find it difficult to relax the vocal tract to the point of being able to produce low notes. From this comes the experience that deep voices (bass and altos) need some time to adjust their vocal tract and its articulation to low notes, because their everyday speaking voice is often higher. Descending warm-ups, therefore, are essential to sing low tones, but sometimes, they may be a hindrance for the absolute depth. Since the focus usually lies on the higher tones, which are more prominent and cause more problems, people rarely focus on warming up the lower tones.

Exercises

Basically, it is possible to sing any exercise that can be sung upwards in a descending way. Usually, just the first note is a problem. Just as it is easier to move from low to high when singing higher notes, the same happens with the deep tones. Exercises where the melodies are sung downwards and where the last note is the deepest are better suited for deep exercises.

Exercise 1

Perform the following exercise in a very relaxed way. Try different vowel positions and do not try to create a uniform vocal colour. The exercise is perfect for loosening the voice.

Variant a)

a) jo   jo   jo   jo
b) ja   ja   ja   ja
c) ju   ju   ju   ju
d) jäi   jäi   jäi   jäi
e) yeah yeah yeah yeah

  Chromatically downwards

Variant b)

a) jo   jo   jo   jo   jo
b) ja   ja   ja   ja   ja
c) ju   ju   ju   ju   ju
d) jäi   jäi   jäi   jäi   jäi
e) yeah yeah yeah yeah yeah

  Chromatically downwards

Variant c)

a) jo   jo   jo   jo   jo
b) ja   ja   ja   ja   ja
c) ju   ju   ju   ju   ju
d) jäi   jäi   jäi   jäi   jäi
e) yeah yeah yeah yeah yeah

  Chromatically downwards

Descending warm-up

Exercise 2

Pay attention to the legato arches in this exercise and note that the last two sounds are metrically stopped. Long tones allow a more effective adjustment to the tone than short tones.

↘ Chromatically downwards

Exercise 3

It often happens that choirs get automatically louder as soon as a tune sequence runs upwards. This is often not wanted.

In the following exercise, it is to be expected that the quarter notes are emphasized. The meter is on beat 1 in the clock, but a too prominent sound should be prevented, which can be tried with the following exercise samples. The pace should be kept quiet.

↘ Chromatically downwards

Exercise 4

Calmly, try to specifically change the articulation. At the beginning, sing with a big awareness of vowels, and in a second phase, specifically pay attention to the consonants. You will notice an impressive difference. Singing on vowels corresponds to a classical vocal setting, but singing on consonants is hardly possible; a balance between the two methods is close to a jazz-pop attitude.

↘ Chromatically downwards

Exercise 5

The following exercise is a good option to do a descending warm-up, but it also activates the diaphragm if the initial vowel P is stressed in variant a).

a) Pa-na-ma, Pa-na-ma, Pa-na-ma, Pa-na-ma, Pa-na-ma

b) Ma-la-ga, Ma-la-ga, Ma-la-ga, Ma-la-ga, Ma-la-ga

↘ Chromatically downwards

Descending warm-up

Exercise 6

Easy descending exercise:

a) wo wa wo wa wo wa wo wa   wo wa wo wa wo
b) a - o - a - o - a - o - a - o   -   a - o - a - o - a

↘ Chromatically downwards

Piano or no piano? – A question of tuning

In many textbooks, we get close to a religious war: Should a choir rehearsal take place with the involvement and support of a piano? One faction vehemently says no, while the other side welcomes it as a good means of support. Ultimately, the answer varies from choir to choir and from the performance practice that always influences dependent rehearsals.

Anyhow, a piano actually affects the voice and the overall sound of a choir, whether it sings in a cappella or is accompanied by a permanent piano. This is largely caused by the so-called *musical tuning*. In simple terms, a sound is a vibration. This is readily apparent when you look at a guitar string. The string vibrates, and the sound is audible. Depending on how the string is touched, different intervals, that are different main tones, will resound. If the string is touched exactly in the middle (1:1) split, we'll have a octave, but if the ratio is 2:3, we'll get a fifth, etc. This type of interval determination is called *just intonation* because of the clear mathematical proportions. This type of interval determination has the disadvantage that if it is transferred to common keyboards, it doesn't permit easy changes of keys.

Every key sounds individually. For this reason, early music composers selected a specific key for each single instrument. Nowadays, the intervals are usually aligned, so we call it a *equal temperament*. The interval ratios are somewhat stretched or compressed, but a change of keys occurs without difficulty. What does this mean for a choir? The human ear is designed differently than a piano and is based on *just intonation*. That means that a choir intones very differently without a piano. Due to these vibrations, it is perfectly natural that a choir falls into intonation during a piece. This is not desirable, but natural. Certain intervals are even intoned slightly differently than in pure intonation in order to be closer to the piano.

This is particularly evident in thirds. As a standard, pianos intone big thirds as too high, small thirds as too low. In *just intonation*, a choir has to intone big thirds in a lower way than small thirds. Only leading tones are an exception, which are classically intoned higher.
In rehearsals, it can be very important to consider if the choir will be accompanied by a piano during the concert.
More information and deeper insight into intonation and the different intonations can be found in any guide book on choirmastership, singing, and music theory.

Incidentally, the various tunings and knowledge of the vibration conditions were already known in ancient times. One of the most famous intonations, the *Pythagorean tuning,* goes back to Pythagoras of Samos, who described the theoretical foundations of music in 500 B.C. Even the so-called, *Pythagorean comma,* the finding that 12 fifths do not mathematically correspond to 7 fifths (System of the circle of fifths), gets its name from him. This difference causes the problem of vibrations in the first place.

VI. Diaphragm activation

The diaphragm and its importance in singing and breathing have already been discussed at length in the chapter on breathing. The following exercises are ideal to activate this muscle band consciously. There are countless exercises on diaphragmatic activation. Common to all of them is the implementation of short and concise bursts using the diaphragm. Many singers find it difficult to concretely focus the diaphragm and to not only use the rest of the abdominal muscles. The following exercises can help you do that. If you put your hands on your stomach, you'll feel the diaphragm and its activity.

Simple exercises in close position

Exercise 1

Variant a)

a) ha ha ha ...
b) he he he ...
c) hi hi hi ...
d) hu hu hu ...
e) mo mo mo ...

↗ Chromatically upwards

Variant b)
Finally, you may optionally insert a bound fifth.

 Chromatically upwards

Exercise 2

The following exercise is modelled on a disco beat. The meter should be consistent throughout the exercise.

 Chromatically upwards

Practical advice: Diaphragmatic activation

Nothing trains the diaphragm better than frequent, abundant and hearty laughing.

Exercise 3

Be careful with the pronunciation. The text is based on the o Italian word *Signora*. *Signora* should be pronounced as [siɲˈnoːɾa].

↗ Chromatically upwards

Exercises in the range of an octave

Exercise 4

Variant a)

a)ha ha ha   ...
b)he he he   ...
c)hi hi hi   ...
d)hu hu hu   ...
e)mo mo mo   ...

↗ Chromatically upwards

Diaphragmatic activation

Variant b)

Optionally, you can add a fifth at the end, once again.

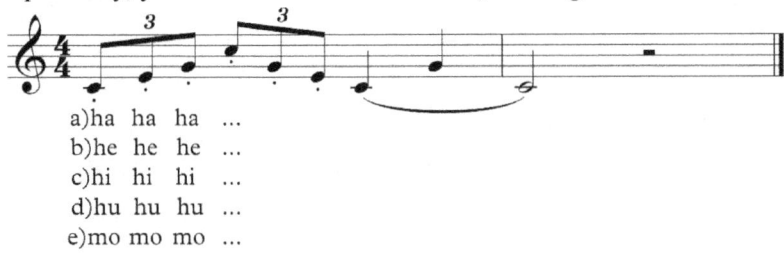

↗ Chromatically upwards

Exercise 5

Variant a)

↗ Chromatically upwards

Variant b)

↗ Chromatically upwards

Diaphragmatic activation

Exercise 6

This exercise is modelled on the famous theme of the aria of the "Queen of the Night" in *The Magic Flute* by Wolfgang Amadeus Mozart. The aria consists of numerous grace notes that are sung over a wide ambit, including even the whistle register, the highest vocal register. These sounds are no longer produced by vibrations of the vocal cords, but by some sort of air turbulence, which is similar to a pipe. However, this register can only be achieved by a few people and hardly matters in a choir.

Imagine the queen and, subsequently, sing the exercise.

Variant a)

a) ha ha ha   ...
b) he he he   ...
c) hi hi hi   ...
d) hu hu hu   ...
e) mo mo mo   ...

↗ Chromatically upwards

Variant b)

a) ha ha ha   ...
b) he he he   ...
c) hi hi hi   ...
d) hu hu hu   ...
e) mo mo mo   ...

↗ Chromatically upwards

Exercise 7

The difficulty of this exercise lies in its length. It is not easy to keep the same suspense over four measures and to sing every note shortly and concisely.

↗ Chromatically upwards

Exercise 8

The following exercise extends over a whole octave and, therefore, should be performed only after the other exercises.

↗ Chromatically upwards

Diaphragmatic activation

VII. Sound and vocal exercises

A good choir is characterized by many single voices that mingle in order to create an overall sound. This overall sound is achieved not least through a common vowel determination. Each vowel can be articulated in the most diverse ways: open, closed, wide, long, front, or in the back. If you manage to set a choir on a common vowel, you will get a lot closer to setting your choir on a common sound. The following exercises should always be considered from the viewpoint of uniform vocal colouring. The vowel sequence a-o-u-e-i often appears in this sense. The reason is that this is the result of a natural transition from lip to jaw closure.

Exercises

Exercise 1

Be careful to colour all vowels in the same way and to perform a gradual passage from one vowel to the next. Pronunciation: [a:] [o:] [u:] [e:] [i:]

↗ Chromatically upwards

Exercise 2

It is often easier to sing a tone with the help of a consonant. For this reason, you should be particularly cautious when intoning the third, which can easily blur without a supportive initial sound.

↗ Chromatically upwards

Exercise 3

Now, it is important to tie the vowels without a new initial tone. Therefore, the Legato should be carried out without restarting each tone. The articulation remains the same; only the pitch changes. In many choirs, an a-ha-ha-ha-ha-ha can be heard instead of a long a [a:]. This often causes very calm and sonorous parts to lose their effect.

↗ Chromatically upwards

Exercise 4

↗ Chromatically upwards

Exercise 5

↗ Chromatically upwards

Exercise 6

The following exercises are great to train the voice with the aid of a soft initial sound. The spelling of the popular jazz notation is adapted. This is how some things should be pronounced:

Whoa = open O [ɔ:]
Whoo = U [u:]
Whee = i [i:]
Whe = e [e:]

Variant a)

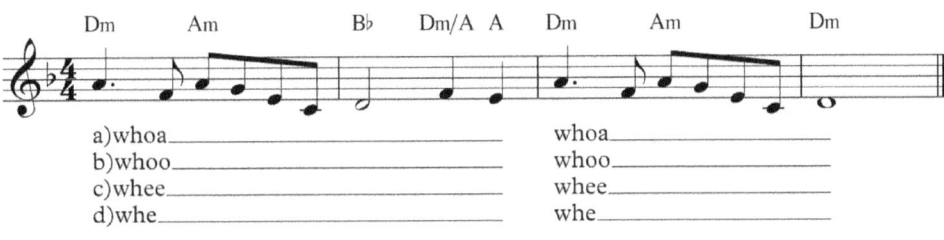

➚ Chromatically upwards

Variant b)

It's all about the contrast between loud and quiet and the brief conclusion on a vowel.

➚ Chromatically upwards

Variant c)

Chromatically upwards

Variant d)

Chromatically upwards

Variant e)

Chromatically upwards

Changing tones chromatically – a simple exercise

Anyone who wants to perform warm-up exercises has to face the problem of having to change the tones chromatically in order to vary the exercises in their pitch. Simple scale exercises still present relatively few problems: You can either only simulate the starting note then sing without accompaniment, or you can simulate an initial chord, which usually is quite unproblematic. Especially with melodic exercises, pop and jazz exercises, and *Groove* practice, which are sung with piano accompaniment, it seems inappropriate, sometimes, if you only lift the basic chord by one level.

Anyhow, there are very easy ways to change a key:

In music, the terms *modulation* or *change* define the slow and initiated change of a key, for example, on common levels of two chords keys. However, when a key is changed abruptly, as is the case when doing warm-up exercises, one speaks of *abrupt modulation*. The simplest form to initiate this process is to simply raise or lower the basic chord by a semitone.

It all gets a bit more elegant if a new target key is introduced. This works in a very simple form with the Dominant Level of the target key with the implied leading tone. A change from C-major to C #-major can be accomplished via G #-major. G #-major is the dominant feature of C #-major. The following tables show the appropriate reconciliation for all twelve pitches by using the dominant chord. The chord notation corresponds, once again, to the international system; B stands for the German H and Bb for the German B:

	1	2	3	4	5	6	7	8	9	10	11	12
Target Key	C C	C# Db	D D	D# Eb	E E	F F	F# Gb	G G	G# Ab	A A	A# Bb	B B
Dominant	G G	G# Ab	A A	A# Bb	B B	C C	C# Db	D D	D# Eb	E E	F F	F# Gb

Sound and vocal exercises

A chromatic passage of C would start at level 1 then jump to the dominant feature of Stage 2 and, thereby, introduce the target key:

C - G# - C# - A - D - A# - D# - B - E - C - F - C# ....

As an example, a possible change from C-major to C#-major:

Another way to create an even more extravagant skidding lies in the introduction of an introductory subdominant with a ninth (dominant) with a bass. Such a chord can also be viewed as an extended derivative action that has the effect of reinforcing the leading tone of the new target key. Such injections are often found in gospel music. A transition from C major to C # -major could look like this:

C - F#/G# - G# - C#

VIII. Polyphonic sound exercises

It is hard enough to complete a clean and effective warm-up program in unison. It is an entirely different matter, however, to warm-up polyphonically. Polyphonically warm-up exercises, primarily, serve sound and intonation education and, therefore, are named like this in this book. As already indicated on several occasions, the greatest art of a choir is to engage all singers and form an overall sound. This applies not only to the vocal timbre and rhythm, which were discussed in the previous chapters. It, particularly, applies to the intonation that is to be trained with the following polyphonic exercises. A uniform rhythm and a single vowel colour are often prerequisites for a clean intonation. The following exercises, therefore, are kept rhythmically simple and are aimed at educating voices. A clean intonation arises when each single person knows his place in singing in harmony and has an idea of the overall sound. Therefore, some exercises for harmony formation should be inserted.

Exercises

At first, let every single voice rehearse individually in the following exercises. Only those who master their own voice can dedicate themselves to choral sound. The mistake that is often made is to give too little attention to individual voices, because they are "only" being warmed up. However, many sound warm-ups can influence the sound of the choir.

Exercise 1: Musical scale exercise

Singing a musical scale is not difficult, especially within the choir. To sing a scale at a certain interval with more voices, at the same time, is a bit harder. The following exercises demonstrate this matter. Any syllable can be taken as timbre. However, it is recommended to use a soft initial sound. Examples can be na, la, mo, nu, o or a

Variant a) Pure fifth

Variant b) Fourth

Variant c) Third

Variant d) Three fourth
The principle also works with several intervals over each other. The feasibility can be limited by the ambit of the singer.

Exercise 2: Tetrads

The following exercise is to train the harmony in the choir as well as the ear. The tetrads are first sung together and then exposed to several voices. The used harmonies often occur both in classical and in modern literature, but hardly as a tune sequence.

Variant a) Pure major chord

Variant b) Major chord with big seventh

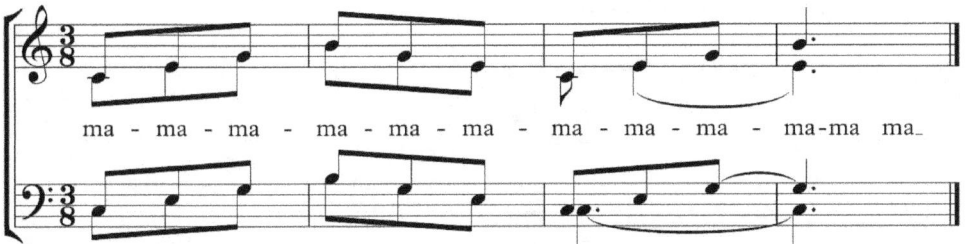

Polyphonic sound exercises

Variant c) Major chord with small seventh

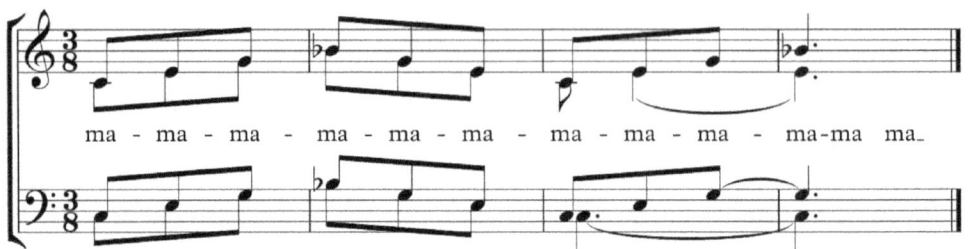

Variant d) Pure minor chord

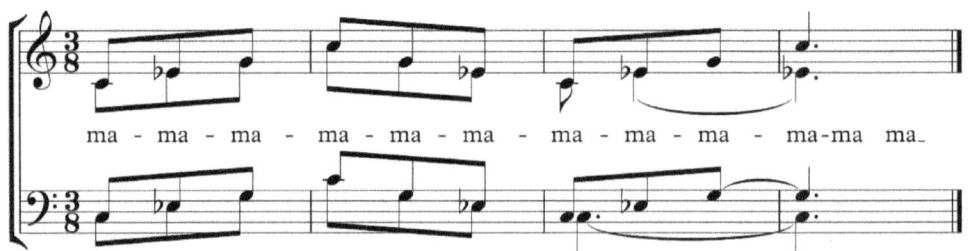

Variant e) Minor chord with small seventh

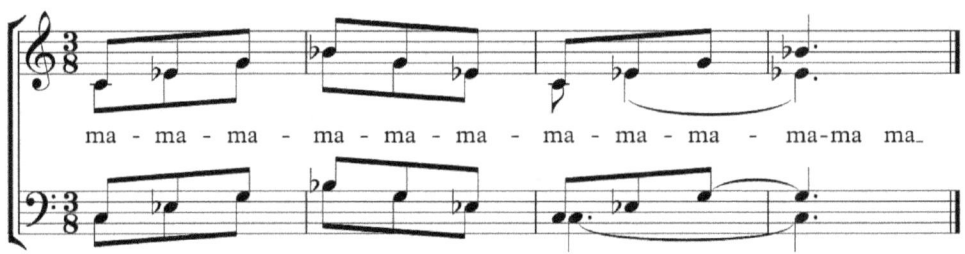

Variant f) Diminished seventh chord

Exercise 3: Tetrads

The following exercise is similar to the previous exercise, but differs in difficulty. In the previous exercise, the tetrad was sung by everybody, first, before being exposed to several voices. In the following exercise, only a fifth is initially sung and then exposed to the tetrad in the course of the exercise. This means the singer must have a clear idea of the chord before he can be suspended without any help. Therefore, the exercise only makes sense if the previous exercise has been practiced several times.

Variant a)
Pure major chord

Polyphonic sound exercises

Variant b)

Major chord with big seventh

Variant c)

Major chord with small seventh

Variant d)

Pure minor chord

Variant e)
Minor chord with big seventh

Variant f)
Minor chord with small seventh

Variant g)
Diminished seventh chord

Exercise 4: Vowel training

The following exercise corresponds to Exercise VII – 2, but it is performed polyphonically. Pay attention to a consistent vowel colouring and a uniform transition.

↗ Chromatically upwards

Exercise 5: Sound and volume training

↗ Chromatically upwards

Exercise 6: Sound of an angel

↗ Chromatically upwards

All about your standing

Warm-ups and the first phase of a choir rehearsal may well be used to try out new methods and techniques. This may also be true for the set-up in a choir. Almost all choirs chose a set-up, which is separated by voices. It does not matter whether the rehearsal takes place in one or two rows. Everybody has their places and their firm parts. This, sometimes, leads the individual hiding behind his part and not accepting any responsibility for his own register. This can be prevented or changed if the formation is varied. Polyphonic warm-up exercises are suitable to this purpose because of their simplicity. The part is not difficult, and after a short repetition, everybody can memorize it, so there aren't any text problems.

In a choir that rehearses in only one row, the following set-ups are the most frequent:

Variant a)

The men's voices are at the centre and are surrounded by the women's voices. This set-up derives from the classic double-breasted line-up and is probably the most common type of set-up.

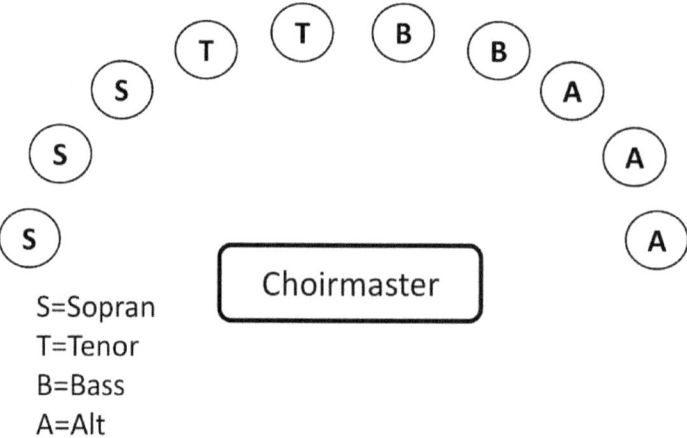

S=Sopran
T=Tenor
B=Bass
A=Alt

Variant b)
The two outer voices (basso and soprano) frame the inner voices.

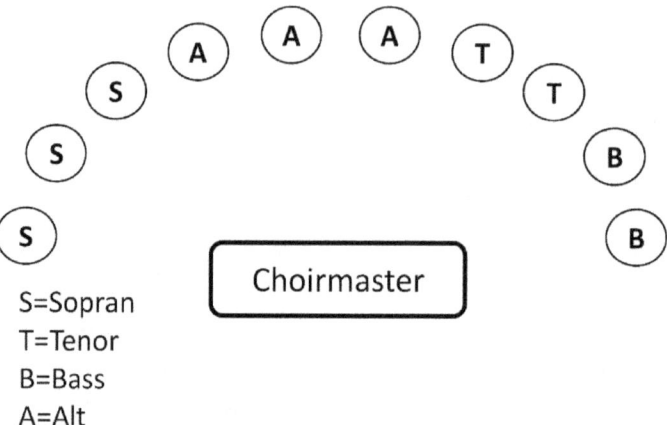

S=Sopran
T=Tenor
B=Bass
A=Alt

Polyphonic sound exercises

In the classical placement of a two-row choir, the female voices are in the front and the men's voices are in the second row.

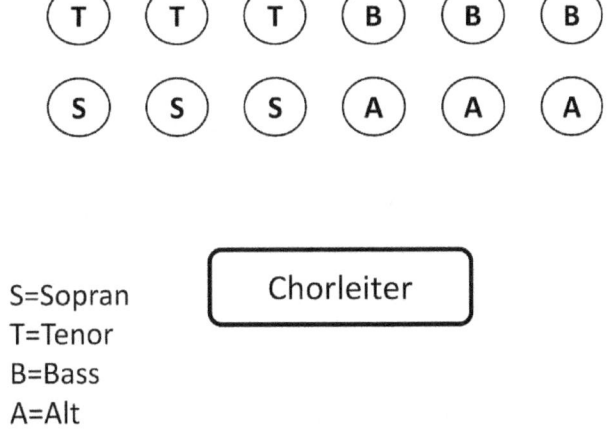

S=Sopran
T=Tenor
B=Bass
A=Alt

In addition to the described variants, there are many other possibilities. However, the described set-ups are the most common.

Changing this placement, once in a while, has many advantages. As already mentioned, choir singers tend to hide behind their own register. If you mix the formation, so everyone stands next to another voice, everyone must sing for themselves and take responsibility. In addition, everyone will hear the other voices and fit better into the overall harmony. When you are warming up, you can easily try this. You will find that the changed set-up always leads to a fuller and deeper sound.

In practice, this method is, particularly, suitable for sections that live off the sound and the harmonies. By mixing voices, you can easily encounter intonation problems. Personal responsibility leads to a more conscious choral sound.

For a two-row choir, a good mixing could look like this:

(T) (B) (S) (A) (T) (B)
(S) (A) (T) (B) (S) (A)

S=Sopran
T=Tenor
B=Bass
A=Alt

Choirmaster

The equivalent in a one-row choir:

(S) (A) (T) (B) (S) (A) (T) (B)

S=Sopran
T=Tenor
B=Bass
A=Alt

Choirmaster

Polyphonic sound exercises

IX. Rounds

Rounds are often known as children's songs or folk songs. On closer examination, however, they stand out as highly complex contrapuntal musical pieces. In addition, they are present in almost any genre, including jazz and classical music. In their pure form, rounds are melodies that imitate themselves through staggered beginnings. This means only a single melody has to be learned in order to sing polyphonically. Therefore, many people choose to sing rounds as a warm-up. The oldest recorded and listed round dates back to England in the 13th century: *Sumer is icumen in* is a six-part piece of music with folk text. Canons probably reached their peak in Baroque music, especially with Johann Sebastian Bach, whose fugues represent a special case of canon and were composed with mathematical precision. Rounds are currently also popular as pop or jazz arrangements in choral singing, which also show publications from bands, like Bertrand Gröger or Oliver Gies. The following exercises are pure canons that are easy to learn and suitable for all ages.

Exercises

Since most rounds are fairly simple and a little complex, the most important thing in canon singing is to have fun and to radiate ease.

Round 1: Fruit round

Round 2: I like the flowers

I like the flowers is an old English song. The simplicity allows for quicker learning. The canon is sing-able by up to four voices. Make sure not to blur the punctures during prolonged singing.

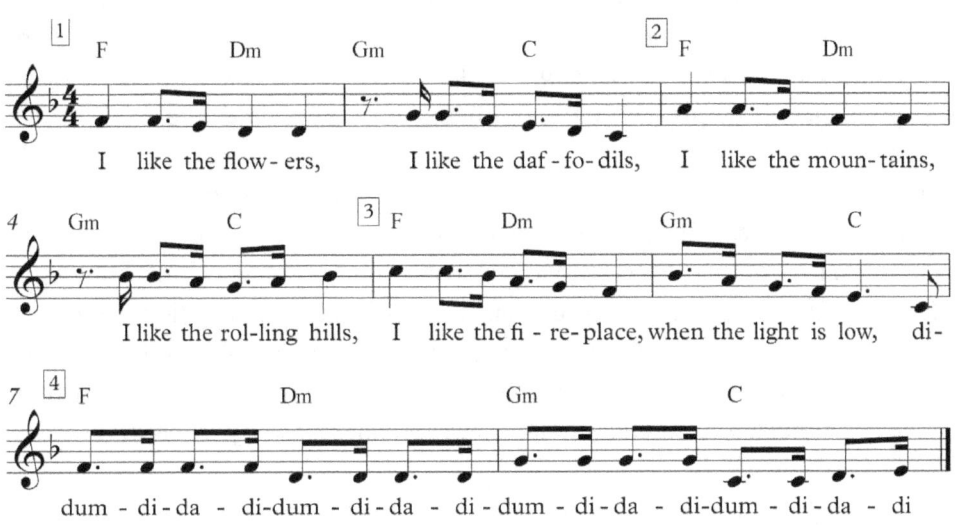

Round 3: Being happy requires a little

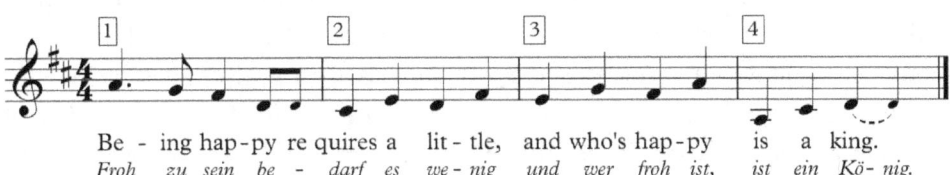

Pronunciation makes the difference

The biggest constant in the evolution of language probably lies in its continuous change.
Language changes from generation to generation, also because it is used as a means of distinction from the previous generation. Although regional languages are repressed by the forms of extensively widespread media, and their transformation is generally slowed, there are still major differences that may cause problems in choral singing. There are numerous books that deal with seemingly *correct* pronunciation. The reasons mentioned above, however, often show that people who work hard to have correct pronunciation, frequently, are the ones that understand the least of the change. This means the following for practice: Agree on a certain pronunciation with your choir and consider regional differences and peculiarities. It's really hard to sing something that is different from everyday language, and people are rarely successful. Especially in unusual or stressful situations, the rehearsed pronunciation is forgotten and everyday language reinstated. You practice intensively on a certain pronunciation and when there is a concert, half the choir will sing something completely different. You should also take into account regional peculiarities.

Regardless of the differences between standard language and everyday language, there is more pronunciation advice that can make many things easier and even help support the choir. As a rule, an expressive sound can be generated only on vowels. This is much more difficulty on consonants. In jazz and pop singing, the opposite is often wanted, and to put this into practice, a great awareness for vocal sound is necessary. For pragmatic reasons, we'll discuss classical vocal training just briefly. If vowels serve sound education, it means that polysyllabic words must always be sung on vowels, and hyphenation is always necessary after vowels. The word *coming* shouldn't be pronounced *com-ing*, but rather separated, like *co-ming*. This rule is generally applicable to all words. The same happens with vowel mutation. Words, like *spoiler,* therefore, can be sung with an open O [ɔ:], which means *spo-iler*. A uniform choir sound and the highest possible sound formation are therefore possible. The individual cases can vary, of course.

Round 4: Shalom chaverim

Shalom chaverim is probably one of the most famous rounds in the German-speaking area. It is an old Israeli folk song, whose author is unknown, as is the case for most folk songs. The song is very calm.

Call-and-Response, printed notes or multimedia?

Warm-up exercises are easy to learn, have simple melodies, and are catchy. At least, this is what I say at the beginning of this book. That this is not always true can be shown, among other things, by the exercises in this chapter. Therefore, not only when doing warm-ups, the question of how to rehearse a piece or an exercise arises. The best known forms are call-and-response, which means singing and having others to repeat, or the classical music editions or copies. Both versions have their advantages and disadvantages. Call-and-response is particularly suitable for catchy melodies, simple texts, and rhythms that are easy to understand. The big advantage lies in the centring of the maestro during the rehearsal, since the singers have no disturbing papers in their hands. In addition, the sound is better, because reading the notes requires a lot of attention. Having free hands and being able to move freely is another pleasant side effect.

Is everything really against the notes? No, notes have their advantages. Call-and-response exercises take time. Time is needed to convey the melody and the text. With notes, the whole process is easier and faster. Even heavy texts or musically difficult passages can be mediated easier. In recent years, increasingly more digital options have reached the market. Nowadays, tablets are frequently used to display notes. The notes are scanned or acquired as PDF documents. The heavy folder and the annoying search for the mentioned passages fall off.

There are numerous apps that display notes and that also have search and archiving functions. PDF documents are usually used, since they work as an excellent screen display. The disadvantage of these functions is the limitation to just one format. It is often difficult to zoom or select special cut-outs that are written with smaller notation. The Spanish app, Blackbinder, which was first presented at the music fair 2014, goes one step further. Blackbinder uses the open file standard MusicXML, which supports the popular music notation software packages (e.g. Sibelius, Finale, Capella, etc.). The app does without the use of thick frames, whereby an almost stepless scaling is possible. In addition, Blackbinder has some useful additional functions. At the beginning, the pace can be entered, which leads to a time-accurate display.

However, this alone would only be a gadget for individual singers if it wasn't for the exciting networking features that are available in the software on top of everything else. Blackbinder is designed to connect different devices. This way, it is possible for the conductor to centrally select the note content, set the pace, and determine the procedure. Each singer then obtains the correct passage on his device. For large choirs or orchestras, an additional voice function can be used, so that loud shouting in a rehearsal room becomes something of the past. However, it is questionable if these software options will spread, since the costs are high and the procedure complex. Presumably, individual solutions will prevail in the near future.

Of course, there are other options in addition to the display via tablet, like the analogical possibility to use printed posters or the digital solution to work with a central projector. Both are a matter of taste and of how much technology is to be used.

Round 5: Much happiness and blessings

The birthday song *Viel Glück und viel Segen* (much happiness and blessings) is quite well-known. Surely, it's less known that it is a wonderful round as well.

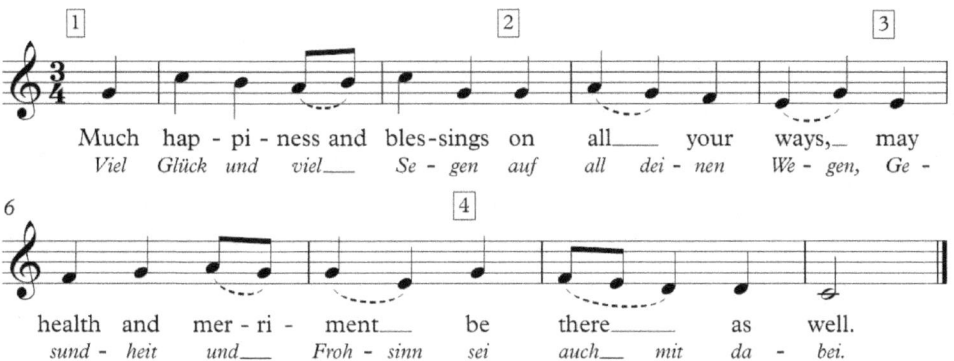

Round 6: Dona nobis pacem

The round, *Dona nobis pacem,* can't be attributed to any author. Although it has been used frequently in history (even by Wolfgang Amadeus Mozart), its utter origin is unknown.

Dona nobis pacem is one of the most melodic and most detailed canons.

Round 7: C O F F E E

The round *C O F F E E Coffee is not for me* is known as a song for kids. However, it is suitable for all ages. The author, Karl Gottlieb Hering (1766-1853), composed other famous rounds in addition to the coffee song. In addition, he might be the possible author of the Christmas carol, *Morgen Kinder wird's was geben.*

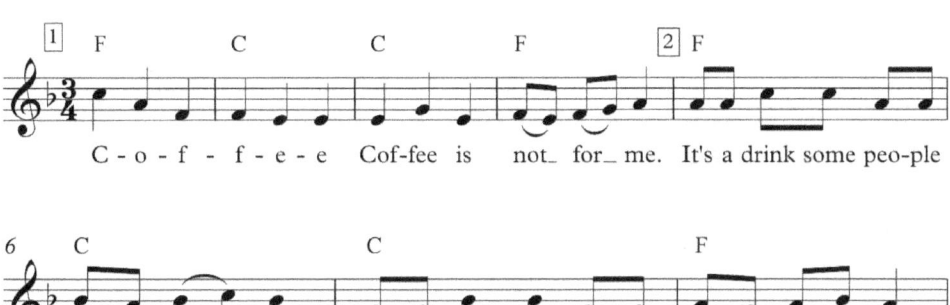

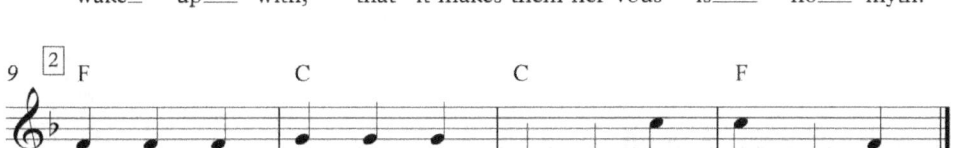

Round 8: Oberammergau

The round *Oberammergau* is a popular song in Germany. The text is very specific therefore it cannot be translated into correct English.

Round 9: Pachelbel-Canon

The following round recreates the famous round in D major by Johann Pachelbel.

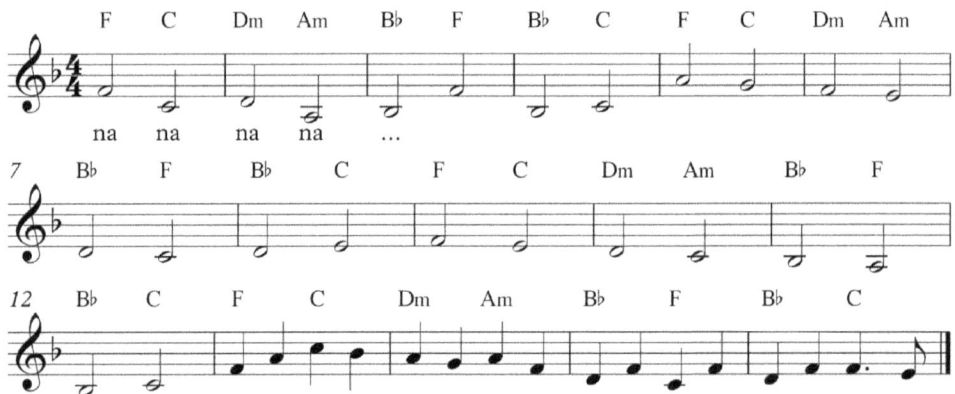

X. Simple popular folk songs

Even if many consider them old-fashioned and out of date, many folk songs exist, and they aren't only known to everyone, but also very convincing from a melodic point of view. This is shown, among other things, by the fact that a lot of folk songs are published in new arrangements and are often covered in the pop / rock genre. They are great to warm-up, primarily, because of their notoriety, their often limited ambit, and the low complexity. Below there are some popular songs that are ideal to warm-up.

Exercises

Practical advice: How to give folk songs a modern twist

Many choral adaptations to folk songs are monophonic. All voices sing the same text at the same rhythm. This often makes those sound quite antiquated for pop / jazz choirs. This sound impression can be easily refreshed if the accompanying voices do not sing the text, but if they perform a sound carpet. The old adaptation is maintained for this purpose, but the text changes into dooh or dah - depending on the occasion. An arrangement can acquire a completely new appearance even when changing the vowel colouring, the metric or the speed. In addition to that, completely new, modern arrangements of traditional songs are often published.

Song 1: The moon has been arising

The Moon has been arising is one of the most famous lullabies in German language. The most famous melody is the reprinted version by Johann A.P. Schulz, but there are over 70 different musical settings to the text, one of which is by Franz Schubert. Even nowadays, the song is continuously released in new versions. In the pop / rock genre, the version by Herbert Grönemeyer, inter alia, is quite known, and he often performs it as the final song of his concerts.

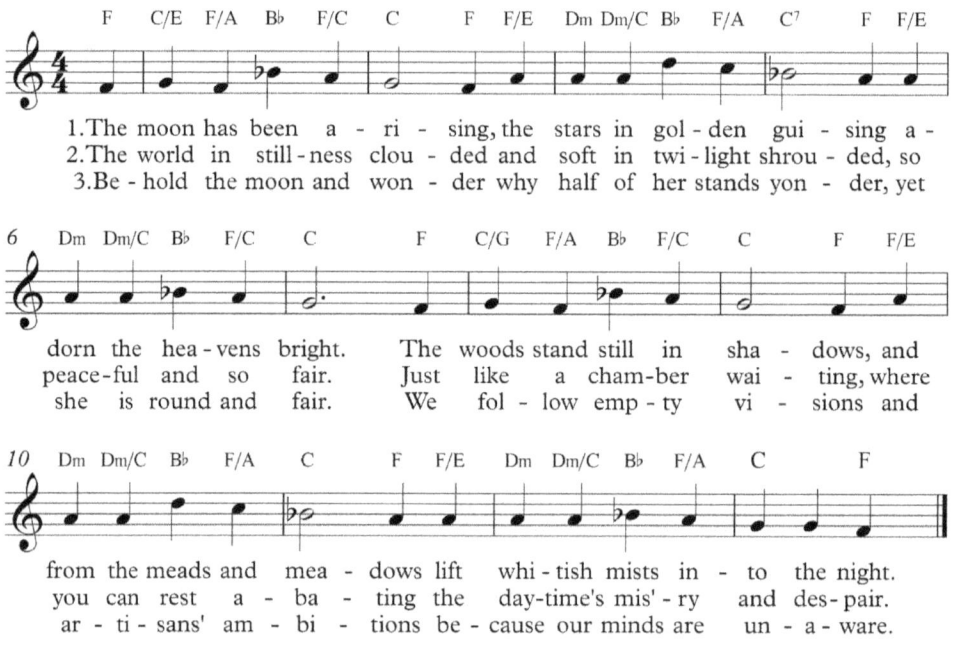

Song 2: Auld Lang Syne

Auld Lang Syne is one of the most popular songs in the English speaking world. It is traditionally sung at the end of the year. It is also known as a farewell song of the worldwide Scout movement. The German punk / rock band Die Toten Hosen has re-interpreted the song, and there are many English-speaking artists who have done the same.

Simple popular folk songs

Song 3: Thoughts are free

The nowadays, well-known text and the melody originated between 1780 and 1830. However, the motive of freedom of thought goes back to ancient times. In German history, the song gained a lot of importance during the revolutionary years.

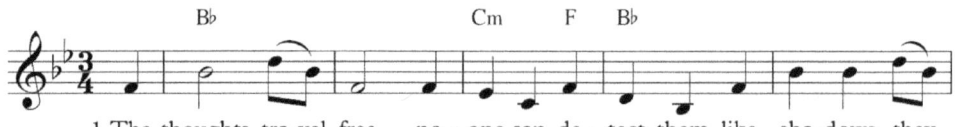

1. The thoughts tra-vel free, no - one can de - tect them, like sha-dows they
2. I think as I choose, my luck's o - pen - end - ded, but all with- out

flee through night to pro-tect them. The cops can not grill them and hun ters can't
clues, so no-one's of - fen - ded. My want and de - si - re shall find no de-

kill them: their guns can not see a thought run ning free.
ni - er when they find the key: That thoughts must be free.

Song 4: Go tell it on the mountain

Go Tell it on the Mountain is an Afro-American gospel, which dates back to the time of the American Civil War. Composer and lyricist are unknown. The song has been covered countless times. The most well-known versions are by Peter, Paul and Mary and Frank Sinatra.

Simple popular folk songs

XI. Generic warm-up sequences

With the large amount of warm-up exercises and the countless categories, it is logical that not all forms and variations can be rehearsed every time. Basically, one has to decide whether it's best to vary the exercises every time the choir rehearses, or if it's a better idea to always use the same sequence and the same exercises. There are choirs that do the same exercises at every rehearsal for a long period of time, so the choirmaster doesn't have to announce the different parts of the warm-up. However, most choirmasters rely on a foundation of various exercises, and they spontaneously pick out a few. Both versions have their advantages and disadvantages. However, it can surely be refreshing to try out a few new exercises from time to time. Below are a few possible warm-up sequences, which are composed of the exercises you found in this book. These sequences are suggestions and can be changed at will. The individual sections, where the exercises were taken, are marked separately for a better orientation.

Possible warm-up: sequence I

Exercise 1: Hang your head

Bend forward and let your head, arms, and torso relax in a hanging position. Please slowly straighten up along your spine. At last, also straighten your head.

Cf.: I – 11, P. 15

Exercise 2: Describe circles with shoulders

Make circles with your shoulders, forward and backwards. Start with the right shoulder first, forward and then backward. Repeat the same exercise with the left shoulder. Then let both shoulders circle together, first forward, then backward. It's quite difficult to circle forward with one shoulder and backwards with the other one.

Cf.: I – 1, P. 11

Exercise 3: Shake off routine

Shake arms and legs. Proceed slowly and decrease the body portion that is to be shaken. For example, first shake the whole arm, then only the hand, and then each single finger. The same can also be done with legs and feet.

Cf.: I – 8, P. 14

Exercise 4: Locomotive

The diaphragm isn't only important during inspiration, but also in exhalation. Especially when singing, the support given by the diaphragm muscle is of great importance.
This can be practiced with short, powerful sounds with a conscious use of the diaphragm. Initially, the variant is "f-s-sh", as it allows a soft start. However, also "p-t-k" is suitable for this exercise.

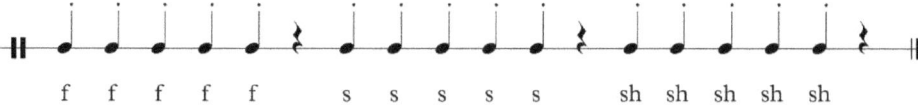

Cf.: II – 5, P. 26

Exercise 5

In order to increase the speed and train the ability in articulating, you can try the following exercise. Start slowly and get faster and faster.

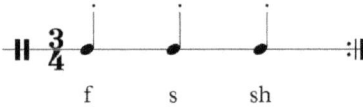

f   s   sh

Cf.: II – 6, P. 27

Exercise 6

Be careful to actually sing Legato during this tone sequence. The single tones shouldn't be hit singularly.

mh_____

↗ Chromatically upwards

Cf.: III – 3, P. 32

Exercise 7

Pay attention to the legato arches in this exercise and note that the last two sounds are metrically stopped. Long tones allow a more effective adjustment to the tone than short tones.

Hal - le - lu - ja

↘ Chromatically downwards

Cf.: VI – 2, P. 55

Exercise 8

The exercise should be carried out in quite a fast pace then become successively faster. The pace is correct if the syllables are still articulated clearly and cleanly.

ma-ma-ni ma-ma-ni ma-ma-ni ma-ma-ni ma

↗ Chromatically upwards

Cf.: IV – 5, P. 37

Exercise 9

The difficulty of this exercise lies in its length. It is not easy to keep the same suspense over four measures and to sing every note shortly and concisely.

a) ha ha ha ...
b) he he he ...
c) hi hi hi ...
d) hu hu hu ...
e) mo mo mo ...

↗ Chromatically upwards

Cf.: VI – 7, P. 64

Exercise 10: Sound and volume training

nu - na - nu - na - nu - na - nu - na - nu - na - nu - na - nu - na - nu   na

↗ Chromatically upwards

Cf.: VIII – 5, P. 80

Exercise 11: Country canon

The following exercise, the *Country canon,* can be used as a canon, as well as a simple, melodic warm-up. Pay attention to the swing rhythm.

↗ Chromatically upwards

Cf.: IV – 18, P. 46

Possible warm-up: sequence II

Exercise 1: The compass

Stretch out your arms on either side of the body and turn them left and right alternately. Important: The feet remain anchored to the floor all the time.

Cf. I – 10, P. 15

Exercise 2: Chew and yawn

Perform comfortable chewing movements. Yawn extensively. Then caress your cheeks and massage your jaw muscles.

Cf. I – 4, P. 13

Exercise 3: Walk on the spot

Start to slowly walk on the spot and become faster and faster, until you're actually running. Get slower and repeat the exercise once more.

Cf. I – 2, P. 12

Exercise 4: Cherry pie with cream

Close your eyes and imagine the delicious smell of a cherry pie with cream. Alternatively, of course, you can think of any other dish that makes your mouth water.

Now, breathe in this soothing smell, deeply through your nose. Change your focus gradually. After you have absorbed the smell twice without instructions, be careful and lead the smell to the abdomen, gradually filling the space of the rib cage, the abdomen and your chest with the smell. All this should happen with the calmness with which you suck in the smell of cherry pie and cream on a quiet Sunday afternoon.

Cf. II – 1, P. 24

Exercise 5: Hard times

Breathe in deeply through your mouth and let the air out with a big, huge sigh. Let your body follow this action by slightly crumpling. Repeat this exercise several times.

Cf. II – 2, P. 24

Exercise 6

Also, this exercise should be sung Legato, without hitting each single tone once again.

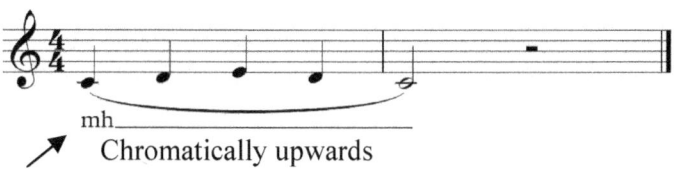

Cf. III – 4, P. 32

Generic warm-up sequences

Exercise 7

Perform the following exercise in a very relaxed way. Try different vowel positions and do not try to create a uniform vocal colour. The exercise is perfect for loosening the voice.

a) jo   jo   jo   jo
b) ja   ja   ja   ja
c) ju   ju   ju   ju
d) jäi   jäi   jäi   jäi
e) yeah   yeah   yeah   yeah

↘ Chromatically downwards

Cf. V – 1, P. 54

Exercise 8: Morning feeling

a) na na na ...
b) la la la ...
c) ma ma ma ...

↗ Chromatically upwards

Cf. IV – 2, P. 36

Exercise 9: Sun

The following exercises should be performed with a lot of sound. Be careful to sing legato on vowels, so they are sung as one, long continuous vowel. Otherwise, it is very easy to transform *Son-ne* or *Sah-ne* in So-ho-ho-honne or Sa-ha-ha-hahne.

 Chromatically upwards

Cf. IV – 11, P. 41

Exercise 10: Sound of an angel

 Chromatically upwards

Cf. VIII – 6, P. 80

Generic warm-up sequences

Possible warm-up: Sequence III

Exercise 1: The compass

Stretch out your arms on either side of the body and turn them left and right alternately. Important: The feet remain anchored to the floor all the time.

Cf. I – 10, P. 15

Exercise 2: Circle your feet

It is not that easy to stand on one leg for a long time. It's even more difficult when you stand on one leg and let the other foot circle around its hinge. Tip: Focus on the little toe of the foot. It helps to maintain the balance.

Cf. I – 7, P. 14

Exercise 3: The pendulum

Oscillate forwards and backwards with your body, as well as to the left and to the right, while standing firmly on the floor.

Cf. I – 3, P. 13

Exercise 4: Balloon

Breathe in deeply, following the above-described pattern, and let the air escape slowly and constantly. The aim is to achieve the longest possible and constant airflow. Measure the time and compare the records to see if there has been an improvement between rehearsals.

The exercise can be performed in different versions on different sounds. Each consonant, thereby, has a different mouth opening and different difficulty.

This exercise seems to work even better when it is performed while lying down. Whoever puts his hand on the abdomen just below the ribs may consciously feel the inhalation.

Cf. II – 4, P. 25

Exercise 5

Also, this exercise should be sung Legato, without hitting each single tone once again.

↗ Chromatically upwards

Cf. III – 4, P. 33

Generic warm-up sequences

Exercise 6

This exercise doesn't only loosen lips and voices, but it also trains the breath and a regular air flow.

Repeat the exercise three times without breathing in the meantime.

a) mo mo mo ...
b) ma ma ma ...

↗ Chromatically upwards

Cf. IV – 6, P. 37

Exercise 7

Perform the following exercise by using the diaphragm.

a) die So, die So, die Son - ne
b) die Sah, die Sah, die Sah - ne

↗ Chromatically upwards

Cf. IV – 10, P. 40

Exercise 8

It often happens that choirs get automatically louder as soon as a tune sequence runs upwards. This is often not wanted.

In the following exercise, it is to be expected that the quarter notes are emphasized. The meter is on beat 1 in the clock, but a too prominent sound should be prevented, which can be tried with the following exercise samples. The pace should be kept quiet.

Chromatically downwards

Cf. V – 3, P. 56

Exercise 9

It is often easier to sing a tone with the help of a consonant. For this reason, you should be particularly cautious when intoning the third, which can easily blur without a supportive initial sound.

Chromatically upwards

Cf. VII – 2, P. 67

Generic warm-up sequences

Exercise 10

The following exercises are great to train the voice with the aid of a soft initial sound. The spelling of the popular jazz notation is adapted. This is how some things should be pronounced:

Whoa = open O [ɔ:]
Whoo = U [u:]
Whee = i [i:]
Whe = e [e:]

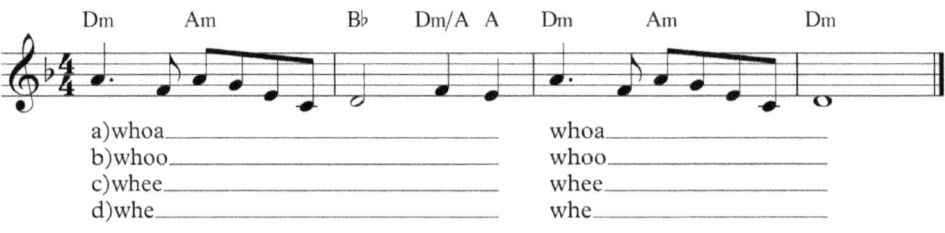

a) whoa
b) whoo
c) whee
d) whe

↗ Chromatically upwards

Cf. VII – 6, P. 69

Warm-up before a performance

It is easy to encounter the statement that warm-ups should be conducted, particularly, intensively before a performance or a concert in order to be perfectly prepared for the upcoming concert. However, this thinking can cause problems. Basically, a warm-up before a concert shouldn't be significantly different from an ordinary warm-up. Extravagant or particularly long warm-ups can unsettle the choir and harm the vocal performance:

1. Do not perform any new exercises to avoid confusing the choir.

2. There should be a strict increase. Even before a concert, the voice needs to be warmed up slowly.

3. Do not overstrain the voices. Also, at a concert, there is no reason to add a new increase to the rehearsals. If rehearsals were conducted systematically and with a target, the maximum has already been reached.

4. Longer does not mean better: Since warm-up exercises can be very energy-demanding, it may happen that this energy could lack at the end of the concert. Extensive coloratura singing or the twentieth diaphragmatic breathing exercise brings no added benefits.

5. Set up rituals: Every person is superstitious, at least in terms of rituals. Avail yourself of this and perform rituals before concerts. The group cohesion and motivation will thank you.

Protect your voice

The cold season is also the most common concert time. This presents a major challenge for our voices. Flu and cold viruses are in the air, and the rooms are warm and dry because of heating. It's easy to be affected by undesirable hoarseness. The following tips will help you protect your voice and allow a rapid regeneration. If your voice is healthy and used normally, however, special protection is usually not necessary:

1. Avoid whispering:
   Many people think that whispering helps conserve the voice. However, the opposite is the case. Whispering stresses the vocal folds much more than soft speaking.

2. No hawking
   Hawking is a habit that many people have and perform unconsciously. However, it is actually dangerous for the voice. If your voice feels a bit weird, try a gentle cough to get it back to normal.

3. Avoid dry rooms
   The dry air of the rooms causes problems to the voice, especially in winter. The warm air causes our mucous membranes to dry out. This is not only a risk factor for annoying colds, but also harms the voice.

4. Drink a lot
   Drinking moistens our throats and allows a physical compensation function when our mucous membranes are dry. However, drink the right drinks. Sage or herbal teas have proven to be very good. Alcohol, however, is counterproductive.

5. Talking is silver, silence is gold
   Talking always strains the voice. Healthy voices do not mind. But if you have a cold or your voice is hoarse, it may be helpful to be quiet. It is said that the Vienna State Opera singers consistently avoid talking before major performances and always carry a notebook to communicate.

6. Avoid spicy sweets
   Many candies contain essential oils, which may corrode the voice. You should, therefore, avoid the widespread eucalyptus candies.

What do professionals think of warming up?

So different the professionals, so different their handling of exercises and warm-ups. Warming up and getting ready is an obvious exercise for many professional choirs and classical singers of opera and theatre.

The situation is different in the field of popular music. Many singers do not warm-up and devote themselves to other preparations. Robbie Williams, for example, needs about five hours to get ready for a concert in order to receive his massages, makeup, and styling. Jeanette Biedermann, however, was known for her extensive warm-ups. Bruno Mars also used to warm-up a lot at the beginning of his career, probably also to counteract the nervousness before concerts. Meanwhile, however, he's also more relaxed about warming up. Once more it shows: The ultimate concept does not exist.

About the author:

Benedikt Lorse, born in 1992, came into contact with choral conducting and performance conduction of musical events during his school days. After he received academic training to become a teacher and then founded his own music publishing company, he devoted himself to advising and supporting amateur choirs. In this book, there are many practical tips from his work as a choirmaster.

www.ingramcontent.com/pod-product-compliance
Lightning Source LLC
Chambersburg PA
CBHW081200230426

43666CB00016B/2877